OCEAN LINERS
OF THE
WORLD

WILLIAM H. MILLER, JR.

© 1984 - William H. Miller, Jr.

ISBN-0-915276-43-7

QUADRANT PRESS, INC.
19 West 44th Street
New York, N. Y. 10036
Phone (212) 819-0822

Early morning arrival at New York of the UNITED STATES, the fastest liner ever built.

Port Authority of New York and New Jersey

INTRODUCTION

Two decades ago, in the early sixties, steamer directories listed over one-hundred deep-sea passenger ship firms that offered ocean transport, passages from Point "A" to Point "B". Today, we tend to forget--- in an age of mass air transport--- that passenger liners ever sold such services. The present cruise business, which has spread throughout the world--- from Bermuda and the Caribbean to the inland rivers of China and even the remote islands of Antarctica--- has replaced those earlier services. Now, only a dozen or so of those previous firms remain in the transportation trades.

The airplane has been the primary reason for this stark changeover. The first commercial jet flew the Atlantic in the fall of 1958 and altered the face of trans-ocean shipping forever. It was a less comfortable but unbeatable offering of 6 hours versus 6 days. The new generation of time- and cost-efficient travelers could no longer afford the indulgence of, say, 5 days to Southampton on the QUEEN MARY or 10 days to Naples on the CONSTITUTION. Quite soon, the liners fell on hard times and into the red. But the sad, rather speedy decline of the North Atlantic liner trades did not

spread quite as rapidly to other, more varied overseas services.

In 1963, tour booklets were still offering extensive combination world cruises by three, four and sometimes five different passenger ships. The process was conveniently packaged. One offering, for example, began at New York with a 5-day crossing on the FRANCE to Southampton. After a brief stay in England, passengers caught the HIMALAYA, a 28,000-tonner of the P&O Lines, from London bound for Sydney via Gibraltar, Palma de Majorca, Naples, Port Said, Aden, Bombay, Colombo, Singapore, Fremantle and Melbourne. Then after a suitable Australian stay, the same tourists could head home to North America aboard Matson's MARIPOSA, sailing from Sydney to San Francisco via Noumea, Suva, Niuafo'ou, Pago Pago and Honolulu. Each of these ships was performing a liner service, carrying passengers from place to place. Cruise passengers were then less of a consideration. Of course, the ships--- with the exception of the MARIPOSA--- were even divided by class: first and tourist for both the FRANCE and HIMALAYA.

Alternately, in that same year, one could take the PRESI-DENT CLEVELAND of the American President Lines across the Pacific, from San Francisco to Honolulu and Yokohama. From that Japanese port, a connection was made with another P&O liner, the ORONSAY, bound for Kobe, Hong Kong, Manila and Sydney. At Australia, the MONTEREY was waiting to return passengers to California via the South Pacific islands and Hawaii. It was all very convenient.

There was even a third possibility: completely around Africa. After crossing on the QUEEN ELIZABETH to Southampton, travelers could head south in the PRETORIA CASTLE, a 747-footer owned by the Union-Castle Line, that called at Madeira, Capetown, Port Elizabeth, East London and Durban. From that latter named port, one could transfer to another Castle liner, the smaller RHODESIA CASTLE, for the homeward run via Lourenco Marques, Beira, Dar-es-Salaam, Zanzibar, Tanga, Mombasa, Aden, Port Said, Naples and then a connection with the Italian CRISTOFORO COLOMBO, which was headed for New York via Genoa, Cannes and Gibraltar.

In those pre-inflationary days, fares for the 70-day world voyage began at $1,510---in first class, no less; $1,598 for the 56-day Pacific circle; and $2,200 for the 75-day Round Africa trip.

Possibly one of the most extensive liner runs was that of the Dutch-flag Royal Interocean Lines, although their ships never went to the home country. Their primary service---carrying three classes of passenger---was from Brazil, Uruguay and Argentina and then across the South Atlantic to South Africa. From there, they proceeded through the Indian Ocean to Malaysia and Indonesia before heading north to Hong Kong, the Philippines and Japan. It was all a casual, almost carefree way of travel---used by tourists, students, old colonials, business types and even exiled royals.

But the jet finally arrived in more distant areas. By the late sixties, there seemed an endless flow of out-of-work, unprofitable passenger ships bound mostly for the scrapyards of Taiwan. Most of them were not replaced. In some cases, even the firms themselves vanished.

By 1972, the cheap junket to places like Singapore and Australia was a killing blow to the likes of the big P&O Lines. Within two years, they scrapped five of their largest liners. The remaining P&O ships turned mostly to cruising, refitted for two-week runs to the Canaries and the Greek isles, Scandinavia and West Africa.

The last major firm to suspend its traditional and historic operations was the Union-Castle Line. In the fall of 1977, the last Castle liners made the final southward passages to the Cape. Jet travel and the change-over to container cargo transport were the primary reasons. At present, South African service from England is maintained by a lone ship, the 8,000-ton CENTAUR, sailing out of Avonmouth for the St. Helena Shipping Company, carrying less than 200 per trip.

On the famed North Atlantic, only Cunard's QUEEN ELIZABETH 2 remains in part-time service to New York and then there are several crossings to Montreal aboard Poland's STEFAN BATORY. Service across the Pacific is even more desolate. Occasionally, P&O sends one of its big ships---usually the 45,000-ton CANBERRA--- on a "positioning trip" via Panama out to Sydney and the South Pacific. It's a once-a-year opportunity as the liner shifts from summer cruising from Britain to winters in Australia.

Freighters were also once a populous and popular form of ocean transport. Most of them carried a dozen or less, thereby avoiding the need to have a doctor onboard as necessitated by international law. These miniature liners offered some of the finest accommodations afloat--- from wood-paneled staterooms that were often twice the size of a first class room on one of the old Cunard QUEENS to gourmet food with rich ethnic overtones. Myself, I can recall living the life of a pampered, sea-going king for 42 days aboard the PRESIDENT TAFT, again of American President Lines. We casually ferried about the Orient---to Yokohama, Kobe, Pusan, Hong Kong and Manila, before returning to California. In 1978, the total fare---for a single cabin, no less---was $1,750.

Today, freighter services with passenger accommodations are almost as uncommon as the old luxury liner trades. It simply doesn't pay---a dozen passengers on large, costly containerships that rarely spend more than a few hours in port.

The remains of the long-ago ocean liner fleets are white-hulled, sleek cruiseships---all one-class vessels that mostly seek warm weather, where the ports are more incidental, more a part of the onboard entertainment and diversion. The changes of the past two decades have been particularly drastic in the passenger ship business.

I have assembled these pages---another work of total joy--- for yet another loving look at the great passenger liners. However, let there be no mistake about it, my intention was not, could not be to include all of the noted firms of the fifties and sixties, those final decades of a vast global passenger ship network. Simply, I have divided this effort into seven chapters: "The North Atlantic Shuttle," "Latin America," "South to Africa," "Local North Sea & Mediterranean Services," "The Soviet Fleet," "The Indian Ocean" and a concluding chapter on "The Pacific," which the P&O Lines once called the "last frontier of modern ocean travel." Representing these varied trade areas are photographs, a good number of which are unpublished previously, that portray some distantly familiar names. Such vessels provided untold magic, romance and inspiration to me.

William H. Miller
Jersey City, New Jersey

QUEEN MARY   Built 1936
Built by: John Brown & Co., Ltd.,
           Clydebank, Scotland
81,237 gross tons   39 foot draft
1019 feet long   119 feet wide
Steam turbines geared to quadruple screw
Service speed 28½ knots
1995 passengers
        711 first class;   707 cabin class
        577 tourist class

[ABOVE] **The majestic and beloved QUEEN MARY outbound for Cherbourg and Southampton passes the Statue of Liberty.**
[OPPOSITE] **Three Cunarders meet in New York. At Pier 92 sits the combination passenger-cargo MEDIA and at Pier 90 are the giant QUEEN ELIZABETH and the more intermediate MAURETANIA. Beyond are the UNITED STATES and the INDEPENDENCE.**

Both photos: Port Authority of New York and New Jersey

THE NORTH ATLANTIC SHUTTLE

CUNARD LINE

In the final heyday of the passenger liner, during the Fifties and Sixties, Britain's Cunard Line was the best known, most distinguished steamship company in the world. In fact, a former purser claimed that "connections" were needed just to be hired. On the North Atlantic, Cunarders carried a third of all passenger traffic as well as the greatest numbers of celebrity clientele — from Hollywood to European royalty, to tycoons and sheiks, prime ministers and presidents. The most illustrious and noted Cunarders were, of course, the QUEEN MARY and QUEEN ELIZABETH. The ELIZABETH was the world's largest liner while the MARY was perhaps the most popular and successful supership ever built. As a weekly team, they maintained the 5-day express run between New York and Southampton, with a stop at Cherbourg en route. The MAURETANIA assisted on a more extended run that included Le Havre and Cobh. The legendary cruise liner CARONIA also made occasional Atlantic trips, often via the Caribbean. The BRITANNIC — the last of the old White Star liners — worked the Liverpool trade to New York via Cobh. She had help from the monthly schedules of the combination ships MEDIA and PARTHIA. To the St. Lawrence, to Quebec City and Montreal, Cunarders sailed from London, Southampton, Liverpool and Greenock in Scotland. Winter trips went to Halifax and sometimes onto New York.

By the time the two QUEENS were retired in 1967-68, Cunard had vastly reduced its traditional Atlantic service and turned mostly to cruising. Now, only the QUEEN ELIZABETH 2 remains, the last of the big North Atlantic liners and the last to sail from New York.

QUEEN ELIZABETH   Built 1940
Built by: John Brown & Co., Ltd.,
                 Clydebank, Scotland
83,673 gross tons   39 foot draft
1031 feet long   119 feet wide
Steam turbines geared to quadruple screw
Service speed 28½ knots
2233 passengers
                823 first class;   622 cabin class
                798 tourist class

First class on the superliner QUEEN ELIZABETH: [ABOVE] The Boat Deck, [LEFT] the Smoking Room and [BELOW] the Main Restaurant. [UPPER RIGHT] For celebrities crossing on the Cunard QUEENS, the glare of public life could be avoided in the Verandah Grill where an extra fee was demanded even of first class passengers. There were usually several noted names aboard each voyage of the famed Cunarders. [LOWER RIGHT] Charles Boyer and Spencer Tracy enjoy a chat aboard the QUEEN MARY in the mid-Fifties.

This page: Herbert G. Frank Jr. Collection. Opposite: Peter Smith Collection, Brenton Jenkins Collection.

UNITED STATES LINES
AMERICAN EXPORT LINES

Yankee colors were carried on the Atlantic by a fleet of modern post-war liners. Most notable was, of course, the brilliant UNITED STATES, the fastest passenger ship ever built. She took the prized Blue Riband from the QUEEN MARY in 1952 with recorded runs of 35-36 knots. The UNITED STATES sailed the Atlantic throughout the year, between New York, Southhampton, Le Havre and sometimes to Bremerhaven. The somewhat smaller AMERICA assisted, but at a more casual pace as she did not have a comparable service speed.

To the Mediterranean, American Export's CONSTITUTION and INDEPENDENCE worked a balance of three-week roundtrips between New York, Algeciras (Spain), Naples, Genoa and Cannes.

The UNITED STATES made the final American-flag passenger crossing on the Atlantic in November 1969.

[ABOVE] **The UNITED STATES arrives at Southampton.** [UPPER RIGHT] **The very beautiful and ever. popular AMERICA sails from New York.** [RIGHT] **The strikingly handsome INDEPENDENCE carried the Stars and Stripes on the Mediterranean run in direct competition with the larger Italian liners.**

Roger Sherlock, Port Authority of New York and New Jersey; Alex Duncan.

UNITED STATES   Built 1952
Built by: Newport News Shipbuilding &
           Drydock Co., Newport News,
           Virginia, USA
53,329 gross tons   28 foot draft
990 feet long   101 feet wide
Steam turbines geared to quadruple screw
Service speed 30-33 knots
1930 passengers
        871 first class;   508 cabin class
        557 tourist class

AMERICA   Built 1940
Built by: Newport News Shipbuilding &
           Drydock Co., Newport News,
           Virginia, USA
33,532 gross tons   29 foot draft
723 feet long   93 feet wide
Steam turbines geared to twin screw
Service speed 22 knots
1046 passengers
        516 first class;
        530 tourist class
      ALSO SEE AUSTRALIS ON PAGE 90

INDEPENDENCE   Built 1951
Built by: Bethlehem Steel Co.,
           Quincy, Massachusetts, USA
30,293 gross tons   30 foot draft
683 feet long   89 feet wide
Steam turbines geared to twin screw
Service speed 23 knots
1000 passengers
        295 first class;   375 Cabin class
        330 tourist class

FRENCH LINE

The French liners had an impeccable, most enviable reputation in Atlantic passenger shipping — prompted in no small way by their superb cooking and luxurious onboard tone. The LIBERTE, ILE DE FRANCE and FLANDRE carried the Tricolor until replaced by the FRANCE, the longest liner ever built, in 1962. Sailings were in direct competition to the Cunard QUEENS and the UNITED STATES — between Le Havre, Southampton and New York. French service ended in 1974, when the FRANCE was laid-up as uneconomic. She was, however, revived five years later as the cruiseship NORWAY.

[ABOVE] **The imposing LIBERTE was the former German speed queen EUROPA of the Thirties. She was given to the French as war reparations in 1946 and then sailed for them on the North Atlantic from 1950 until 1961. She finished her days at the scrapyards of La Spezia, Italy.** [UPPER RIGHT] **The modernistic FRANCE, with her winged, smoke-deflector funnels, was the last liner built for the French Line. She was also the very last supership intended to spend most of her days on the transatlantic run. Put out of work twelve years after her maiden run, she now sails in the Caribbean as the NORWAY. At present, she ranks as the largest liner afloat.**

French line: Roger Sherlock

LIBERTE   Built 1930
Built by: Blohm & Voss A/G,
               Hamburg, Germany
51,839 gross tons   34 foot draft
936 feet long   102 feet wide
Steam turbines geared to quadruple screw
Service speed 24 knots
1502 passengers
          555 first class;   497 cabin class
          450 tourist class

FRANCE   Built 1962
Built by: Chantiers de l'Atlantique
               St. Nazaire, France.
66,348 gross tons   34 foot draft
1,035 feet long   110 feet wide
Steam turbines geared to quadruple screw
Service speed 30 knots
1944 passengers
          501 first class;   1,443 tourist class

to
EUROPE
by
FRENCH LINE

WORLD'S LARGEST LINERS PAST & PRESENT

Gross Tonnage	Ship	Length	Owner
83.673	QUEEN ELIZABETH	1,031'	Cunard
82.799	NORMANDIE	1,029'	French Line
81.237	QUEEN MARY	1,019'	Cunard
70.202 [66.348]	*NORWAY [ex-FRANCE]	1,035'	Norw-Carribean French
67.107	*QUEEN ELIZABETH 2	936'	Cunard
59.957 [54.282]	LEVIATHAN [ex-VATERLAND]	950'	US Lines Hamburg American
56.551 [54.300]	MAJESTIC [ex-BISMARK]	956'	White Star Hamburg American
53.329	UNITED STATES	990'	US Lines
52.226 [51.969]	BERENGARIA [ex-IMPERATOR]	919'	Cunard Hamburg American
51.839 [49.746]	LIBERTE [ex-EUROPA]	936'	French Line N'German Lloyd
51.656	BREMEN	938'	N'German Lloyd
51.062	REX	879'	Italian Line
48.502	CONTE DI SAVOIA	814'	Italian Line
48.158	BRITANNIC	903'	White Star
48.000	**JUBILEE	750'	Carnival Cruise
48.000	**CELEBRATION	750'	Carnival Cruise
46.349	OLYMPIC	882'	White Star
46.329	TITANIC	882'	White Star

* Denotes ship presently in service.

Gross Tonnage	Ship	Length	Owner
45.933	RAFFAELLO	902'	Italian Line
45.911	MICHELANGELO	902'	Italian Line
45.733	*CANBERRA	818'	P&O [P&O Orient]
45.000	**ROYAL PRINCESS	754'	P&O-Princess
45.000	**HOLIDAY	750'	Carnival Cruise
43.153	ILE DE FRANCE	791'	French Line
42.512	L'ATLANTIQUE	742'	Cie Sud-Atl'que
42.348	EMPRESS OF BRITAIN	758'	Canadian Pacific
41.923	*ORIANA	804'	P&O [P&O Orient]
39.241	*OCEANIC	782'	Home Lines
38.645	*ROTTERDAM	748'	Holl-America
38.175	*FESTIVALE [ex-S.A. VAAL, [exTRANSVAAL CASTLE	760'	Carnival Cruise
38.000	*FAIRSKY	790'	Sitmar
37.640	WINDSOR CASTLE [now renamed MARGARITA L]	783'	Union Castle
37.600	*SONG OF AMERICA	703'	Royal Carib Cruise
36.982	NIEUW AMSTERDAM	758'	Holl-America
36.700	*TROPICALE	671'	Carnival Cruise
36.000	**unnamed superferry	580'	Viking Line
35.655	MAURETANIA	772'	Cunard

** Denotes ship presently under construction.

After the Second World War there seemed to be little that reflected the LIBERTE's earlier life as the German greyhound EUROPA. She was unmistakably transformed into yet another great French Line ship with high living on the high seas. The magnificent interiors of the French Line's LIBERTE: [ABOVE] The First Class Gallery, [LEFT] the Library, [LOWER LEFT] the Smoking Room, [UPPER RIGHT] the sitting room of the Alsace Suite, [RIGHT] the children's play-room and [LOWER RIGHT] the indoor pool.

All photos: Herbert G. Frank, Jr. Collection

Trench
Line

HOLLAND AMERICA LINE

The Dutch on the North Atlantic presented a strong, sturdy and spotless image. The ROTTERDAM (the first Atlantic liner to do away with the conventional smokestack), the exquisite NIEUW AMSTERDAM and the tourist-oriented STATENDAM created the "Big Three" — sailing from New York each Friday afternoon for Southampton, Le Havre and Rotterdam. The sisters RYNDAM and MAASDAM — largely responsible for the emergence of the tourist-class liner — traded on a more extended schedule that included Cobh or Galway in Ireland and later to Bremerhaven. Sailings were also offered to Montreal and Quebec City. The combo liners NOORDAM and WESTERDAM ran a monthly service, with 9-day sailings in each direction, between Rotterdam and New York.

Holland-America turned completely to cruising in more recent years and closed down its Atlantic service in 1971.

NIEUW AMSTERDAM   Built 1938
Built by: Rotterdam Drydock Company,
                Rotterdam, Holland.
36,982 gross tons   31 foot draft
758 feet long   88 feet wide
Steam turbines geared to twin screw
Service speed 21 knots
1157 passengers
           574 first class;   583 tourist class

ROTTERDAM   Built 1959
Built by: Rotterdam Drydock Company,
                Rotterdam, Holland.
38,645 gross tons   29 foot draft
748 feet long   94 feet wide
Steam turbines geared to twin screw
Service speed 20½ knots
1356 passengers
           301 first class;   1055 tourist class

[LEFT] Double header: the NIEUW AMSTERDAM and ROTTERDAM are together in drydock at Rotterdam for their annual overhauls. [ABOVE] The STATENDAM — built primarily for the Atlantic tourist class trade — was considered by ship appraisers to be one of the finest looking vessels of the Fifties. [BELOW] The RYNDAM and her sistership MAASDAM ushered in the age of tourist class dominance aboard post-war transatlantic liners. On these ships, the tourist section occupied some 90% of the shipboard spaces, leaving a mere penthouse area for a token first class with 39 berths.

Opposite: Herbert G. Frank, Jr. Collection. This Page: Roger Sherlock.

STATENDAM   Built 1957
Built by: Wilton - Fijenoord Shipyard,
                Schiedam, Holland
24,294 gross tons
642 feet long   81 feet wide
Steam turbines geared to twin screw
Service speed 19 knots
952 passengers
          84 first class;   868 tourist class

RYNDAM   Built 1951
Built by: Wilton - Fijenoord Shipyard,
                Schiedam, Holland
15,015 gross tons
503 feet long   69 feet wide
Steam turbines geared to single screw
Service speed 16½ knots
878 passengers
          39 first class;   839 tourist class

Mild weather crossings on the North Atlantic: [ABOVE] **The Sports Deck onboard the RYNDAM and** [RIGHT] **the open promenade on the STATENDAM.**

Both photos: Herbert G. Frank, Jr. Collection.

Bouillon at eleven and tea at four — a carefree relaxing day on deck aboard the RYNDAM.

Holland-America Line
s.s. STATENDAM

"It's good to be on a well-run ship"

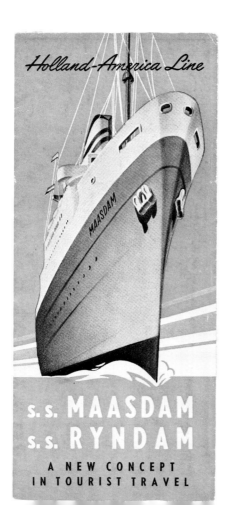

Holland-America Line

s.s. MAASDAM
s.s. RYNDAM

A NEW CONCEPT
IN TOURIST TRAVEL

ITALIAN LINE

The Italian Line had enormous popularity --- prompted, among other reasons, by the year-round warm-weather climate of the mid-Atlantic. Passenger services were divided between two distinct routings: the express run between Naples, Genoa, Cannes, Gibraltar and New York --- which was handled by the ANDREA DORIA and CRISTOFORO COLOMBO, later the LEONARDO DA VINCI (the replacement for the ill-fated DORIA) and finally by the MICHELANGELO and RAFFAELLO; and the more extended operation from Trieste and Venice to New York via Dubrovnik, Patras (in Greece), Palermo, Messina, Naples, Barcelona and Lisbon, which was worked primarily by the motorliners SATURNIA and VULCANIA. Italian liners also put into Halifax on many westbound crossings (to land Canadian immigrants mostly) and, on occasion, at Boston on the outbound runs.

The LEONARDO DA VINCI made the last Italian Atlantic crossing in 1976.

LEONARDO DA VINCI   Built 1960
Built by: Ansaldo Shipyard,
                 Genoa, Italy
33,340 gross tons
761 feet long   92 feet wide
Steam turbines geared to twin screw
Service speed 23 knots
1326 passengers
          413 first class;   342 cabin class
          571 tourist class

ANDREA DORIA   Built 1953
Built by: Ansaldo Shipyard,
                 Genoa, Italy
29,083 gross tons
700 feet long   90 feet wide
Steam turbines geared to twin screw
Service speed 23 knots
1241 passengers
          218 first class;   320 cabin class
          703 tourist class

[LEFT] **The magnificent LEONARDO DA VINCI — another beautifully proportioned Italian Liner — was commissioned in the summer of 1960 and was designed to be converted to nuclear propulsion. Of course, this never came to pass.** [ABOVE] **The motorliners SATURNIA and her near-sister VULCANIA were the most profitable post-war Italian liners on the North Atlantic. They carried tens of thousands of immigrants to both Halifax and New York, consequently making millions for their owners.** [BELOW] **The ANDREA DORIA — commissioned in January 1953 as the post-war flagship of the entire Italian merchant marine — is assuredly best remembered for her tragic end. After a collision with the Swedish liner STOCKHOLM off Nantucket on July 25th 1956, she sank in the early morning hours of the next day. There were 52 casualties in this widely publicized disaster.**

Port Authority of New York and New Jersey; Alex Duncan; World Ship Society Collection.

SATURNIA   Built 1927
Built by: Cantieri Navali Triestino,
                    Monfalcone, Italy
24,346 gross tons
630 feet long   80 feet wide
Sulzer diesel geared to twin screw
Service speed 19 knots
1479 passengers
            255 first class;   270 cabin class
            954 tourist class

NORTH GERMAN LLOYD

The first German liner on the Atlantic after the Second World War was the BERLIN, the former Swedish GRIPSHOLM (1925), which was added in 1954. She sailed for the North German Lloyd and, within five years, was joined by the much larger BREMEN. Very high standard Atlantic service was provided between Bremerhaven, Southampton, Cherbourg and New York. This trade remained until 1971, when NGL decided to concentrate only on cruising.

Other Germans on the Atlantic included the Hamburg-Atlantic Line, which added the HANSEATIC in 1958, and the Europe-Canada Line's SEVEN SEAS, a ship particularly popular with students and immigrants.

North German Lloyd's BREMEN of 1959 was actually converted from the French troopship PASTEUR, built in 1939.

North German Lloyd.

BREMEN   Built 1939
Built by: Chantiers de l'Atlantique,
                St. Nazaire, France
32,336 gross tons
697 feet long   88 feet wide
Steam turbines geared to quadruple screw
Service speed 23 knots
1122 passengers
            216 first class;   906 tourist class

ALSO SEE PASTEUR ON PAGE 79

SHIPPING—MAILS

ALL HOURS GIVEN IN DAYLIGHT SAVING TIME

Ships That Arrived Yesterday

Ship	From	Date
QN. OF BERMUDA	Bermuda	Sept. 23
OCEAN MONARCH	St. Maarten	Sept. 21
SANTA PAULA	Port au Prince	Sept. 21
*SUNIMA	Philadelphia	Sept. 24
*SIDONIA	Philadelphia	Sept. 24
*TEXACO NO. DAK.	Port Arthur	—
*CROWN TRADER	Houston	—
*ENTERPRISE	Puerto la Cruz	—
*DEGANYA	Yokohama	—
*RAPHAEL SEMMES	Ponce	—
*ARTLENBURG	La Ceiba	—
*TURANDOT	Cristobal	—
*ERIK BLUMENFELD	Los Angeles	—
*HARMONY	El Palito	—
*SOCONY VACUUM	Beaumont	—
*P. C. SPENCER	Houston	—
*MORMACISLE	Baltimore	Sept. 24
TEXACO NO. CARO.	Port Arthur	—
JAMUNDA	Punta Cardon	—
JALADHRAN	Boston	Sept. 24
BELOIT 'VICT	Bridgeport	Sept. 24
PARISMINA	Armuelles	—
CIT. SERV. BALTI	Lake Charles	—
SAN FRANCISCO	Jacksonville	—
NORDHVAL	Philadelphia	Sept. 24
HONDURAS	Champerico	—
CIBAO	Puerto Plata	—
BARBARA	New Orleans	—
SAXONIA	Norfolk	—
BIENVILLE	Houston	—
SOESTDYK	Norfolk	—
ASTRID NAESS	Amuay Bay	—
MONTEVIDEO	Newport News	—
NANDO FASSIO	Norfolk	—
TEXACO OKLA	Philadelphia	Sept. 24
TEMERAIRE	Camden	Sept. 24
CHERRY VALLEY	Houston	—
SKIENSFJORD	Bergen	—
ESSO CHILE	Aruba	—
SEATR. LOUISIANA	Texas City	—
CALDAS	Jacksonville	—
KEYSTONE STATE	Philadelphia	Sept. 24
LUNA MAERSK	Boston	Sept. 24
LECHSTEIN	Bremen	—
YAKA	Norfolk	—
AWAJISAN MARU	Casablanca	—
GLENVILLE	Bremerhaven	—
GUADALUPE	Houston	—
ADARA	Norfolk	—
OAKVILLE	Suez	—
ASHTARAK	Punta Cardon	—

*Arrived late Thursday.

Incoming Passenger and Mail Ships

Today, Sept. 26 6 4

Ship	Passengers	From	Due	Will Dock
HOMERIC, Home	(614)	Nassau, Sept. 23	8 A.M	W. 57th St.

Tomorrow, Sept. 27

SANTA LUISA, Grace	(12)	Fort de France, Sept. 23	8 A.M	W. 15th St.

Monday, Sept. 28

KUNGSHOLM, Swed. Amer.	(555)	Goeteborg, Sept. 19	1:30 P.M	W. 57th St.
CARONIA, Cunard		Ponta Delgada, Sept. 23	8 A.M.	W. 52d St.
MAASDAM, Holl.-Amer.	(506)	Bremerhaven, Sept. 17	1 P.M	W. Houston St.
WESTERDAM, Holl.-Amer.	(77)	Rotterdam, Sept. 19	Noon	W. Houston St.
WILLEM RUYS, Holl.-Amer		Pt. Everglades, Sept. 26	8 A.M	W. Houston St.
SANTA ISABEL, Grace	(12)	Cristobal, Sept. 16	8 A.M	W. 15th St.
SANTA MARIANA, Grace	(41)	Cristobal, Sept. 23	8 A.M	Port Newark, N. J.

Tuesday, Sept. 29

QUEEN MARY, Cunard	(991)	Southampton, Sept. 24	P.M	W. 52d St.
BREMEN, No. German Lloyd	(923)	Bremerhaven, Sept. 22	1 P.M	W. 48th St.
GEN. S. B. BUCKNER, Mil. Tr.	(1,270)	Bremerhaven, Sept. 21	8 A.M	[illegible] St., Bklyn.

Wednesday, Sept. 30

FRANCE, French		Havre, Sept. 25	A.M	W. 48th St.
INDEPENDENCE, Amer. Export		Genoa, Sept. 18	8 A.M	W. 44th St.
NIEUW AMSTERDAM, Holl.-Amer		Rotterdam, Sept. 22	8 A.M	W. Houston St.
SANTA ROSA, Grace	(170)	Kingston, Sept. 26	8 A.M	Port Newark, N. J.

Thursday, Oct. 1

L. DA VINCI, Italian		Genoa, Sept. 22		W. 50th St.
SYLVANIA, Cunard		Liverpool, Sept. 23		W. 52d St.
GEIGER, Mil. Tr		San Juan, Sept. 27		58th St., Bkln.

Friday, Oct. 2

QUEEN OF BERMUDA, Furness		Bermuda, Sept. 30		W. 55th St.

West Coast Military Arrivals

Ship	From		Will Dock
GEN. D. I. SULTAN	Yokohama, Sept. 13	San Francisco	Sept. 26
GEN. WM. MITCHELL	Honolulu, Sept. 24	San Francisco	Sept. 29
GEN. E. D. PATRICK	Subic Bay, Sept. 19	San Francisco	Oct. 9
GEN. W. A. MANN	Yokohama, Sept. 28	San Francisco	Oct. 12
JOHN C. BRECKINRIDGE	Honolulu, Oct. 10	San Francisco	Oct. 17
BARRETT	Yokohama, Oct. 7	San Francisco	Oct. 21
GEN. H. J. GAFFEY	Subic Bay, Oct. 13	San Francisco	Oct. 31

Ships That Departed Yesterday

Ship	Destination	Date
SANTA ELENA	Fort de France	Oct. 13
*SEATRAIN N. J.	San Juan	—
*HOEISAN MARU	Philadelphia	Sept. 25
*HORNCAP	Curacao	—
*BLACK TERN	Antwerp	—
*RAVENSBERG	Boston	Sept. 25
*BLACK EAGLE	Boston	Sept. 25
*ARGENTINA	Oslo	—
*GERMA	Chandler	—
*ANADARA	Curacao	—
*HEWELIUSZ	Philadelphia	Sept. 25
*MORAZAN	Puerto Cortez	Oct. 6
*ALOR STAR	Pointe a Pierre	—
*SUNRANA	Smalkalden	—
*ALAMAK	Beirut	—
*GATEWAY CITY	Baltimore	Sept. 25
*PIONEER TIDE	St. Nazaire	—
GYPSUM EMPRESS	Hantsport	—
ETUDE	Coatzacoalcos	—
RAUHAEL SEMMES	San Juan	Sept. 29
SELMA THORDEN	Philadelphia	Sept. 26
HOEGH GANNET	Aruba	—

*Sailed late Thursday.

Outgoing Passenger and Mail Ships

SAILING TODAY

Trans-Atlantic

AFRICAN MOON (Farrell), Monrovia Oct. 6, Abidian 10, Tema 12, Duala 15 and Lagos 23; sails from 35th St., Brooklyn.

NORDHVAL (Black Diamond), Dakar Oct. 6, Monrovia 10, Abidjan 11, Pointe Noire 18, Libreville 21 and Duala 23; sails from Court St., Brooklyn.

UPSHUR (Military Transport), Bremerhaven Oct. 5; sails 2 P.M. from 58th St., Brooklyn.

South America, West Indies, Etc.

HOMERIC (Home), Nassau Sept. 29; sails 4 P.M. from W. 57th St.

OCEAN MONARCH (Furness), West Indies Cruise; sails 3 P.M. from W. 55th St.

QUEEN OF BERMUDA (Furness), Bermuda Sept. 28; sails 3 P.M. from W. 55th St.

SANTA MERCEDES (Grace), Santa Marta Oct. 1, Cartagena 2, Cristobal 3, Buenaventura 5, Guayaquil 7 and Callao 9; sails 5 P.M. from Port Newark, N. J.

SANTA PAULA (Grace), Curacao Sept. 30, La Guayra Oct. 1, Aruba 2 and Port au Prince 5; sails 5 P.M. from W. 15th St.

SAILING TOMORROW

South America, West Indies, Etc.

FAIRLAND (Sea-Land), San Juan Oct. 1; sails from Elizabeth, N. J.

SAILING MONDAY, SEPT. 28

Trans-Atlantic

FINNTRADER (Boise-Griffin), Helsinki Oct. 13; sails from Java St., Brooklyn.

STEEL DESIGNER (Isthmian), Alexandria Oct. 15, Massawa 23, Dammam 29, Khorramshahr Nov. 3 and Basra 7; sails from Erie Basin, Brooklyn.

South America, West Indies, Etc.

ADARA (Black Diamond), Asuncion Oct. 27; sails from Court St., Brooklyn.

LATER SAILINGS

Tuesday, Sept. 29

TRANS-ATLANTIC

Exbrook (Amer. Export)	Genoa
Fernland (Barber)	Freetown
Hellenic Beach (Hellenic)	Latakia
Siletta (Funch, Edye)	Penang
S. of U. Pradesh (Norton Lilly)	Aden
Amer. Chieftain (U. S. Lines)	Havre
Amer. Scientist (U. S. Lines)	Havre
Amer. Scientist (U. S. Lines)	Dublin
Willem Ruys (Holl.-Amer.)	Rotterdam

SOUTH AMERICA, WEST INDIES, ETC.

Corsair (Atlantic	Antigua
Havhok (Alcoa)	Guanta
Ice Flower (Atlantic)	St. Kitts
Mormacdawn (Moore-McCormack)	Trinidad
Mormacpride (Moore-McCormack)	Buenos Aires

Wednesday, Sept. 30

TRANS-ATLANTIC

Blankaholm (Swed. Amer.)	Goeteborg
Bremen (No. German Lloyd)	Bremerhaven
Concordia Sky (Boise-Griffin)	Latakia
Dettisfoss (A. L. Burbank)	Reykjavik
Expeditor (Amer. Export)	Bombay
Gen. A. M. Patch (Mil. Tr.)	Bremerhaven
Hellenic Destiny (Hellenic)	Goeteborg
Independence (Amer. Export)	Genoa
Maasdam (Holl.-Amer.)	Bremerhaven
Mormacbay (Moore-McCormack)	Oslo
Queen Mary (Cunard)	Southampton
Selma Thorden (Boise-Griffin)	Goeteborg
Skiensfjord (Norw. Amer.)	Oslo

SOUTH AMERICA, WEST INDIES, ETC.

C. de Pereira (Grancolohbiana)	Buenaventura
Cd. de Popayan (Grancolombiana)	Pto. Limon
Kungsholm (Swed. Amer.)	West Indies
San Juan (Sea-Land)	San Juan
Santa Isabel (Grace)	Cristobal
Santa Luisa (Grace)	S. Domingo
Santa Mariana (Grace)	Nassau
Santo Cerro (United Fruit)	Pto. Cortez

Thursday, Oct. 1

TRANS-ATLANTIC

Caronia (Cunard)	Mediterranean
France (French)	Havre

Friday, Oct. 2

TRANS-ATLANTIC

L. da Vinci (Italian)	Genoa
Sylvania (Cunard)	Liverpool
Westerdam (Holl.-Amer.)	Rotterdam

SOUTH AMERICA, WEST INDIES, ETC.

N. Amsterdam (Holl.-Amer.)	West Indies

Foreign Port Arrivals

Ship	At	Date
L. DA VINCI	Gibraltar	Sept. 25
SATURNIA	Lisbon	Sept. 25
VULCANIA	Barcelona	Sept. 25
C. COLOMBO	Gibraltar	Sept. 25
OSLOFJORD	Oslo	Sept. 25
ARGENTINA	Rio de Janeiro	Sept. 25
AMERICA	Havre	Sept. 25
PRES. POLK	Bombay	Sept. 25
SANTA MARIA	Cristobal	Sept. 25

Cargo Ships Duc Today

Ship	From	Will Dock
AMER. CHIEF	Norfolk	A T, Bn
AMER. FORWARDER	Baltimore	A T, Bn
ATL. SEAMAN	Pilottown	Perth Amboy
CORDOBA	Marseilles	7, B T, Bn
ESSO CANTERBURY	Amuay Bay	Con Hook
FAIRLAND	San Juan	Elizabeth
GYPSUM PRINCE	Hantsport	Stoney Point
HONOLULU MARU	Yokohama	39 St, Bn
IVERNIA	Liverpool	94, N R
OVERO	Rio de Jan	29 St, Bn
PIA COSTA	Leghorn	E B T, Bn
PIONEER MIST	Norfolk	A T, Bn
PIONEER MOON	London	—
ROBIN LOCKSLEY	Baltimore	23 St, Bn
STEEL SEAFARER	Alicante	Isth EBT, Bn

Outgoing Freighters

Ship	Destination	Date
KEYSTONE STATE	Havre	Sept. 26
SEATRAIN N. Y	San Juan	Sept. 26
COLORADO	Naples	Sept. 27
STEEL NAVIGATOR	Manila	Sept. 27
EXFORD	Riveka	Sept. 28
LANCASHIRE	Sydney	Sept. 28
LOIDE CHILE	Santos	Sept. 28
TEMERAIRE	Manila	Sept. 28
BLACK HERON	Antwerp	Sept. 28
ANNA ISABEL	Puerto Limon	Sept. 28
PIONEER MIST	Manila	Sept. 28
IRISH POPLAR	Dublin	Sept. 28

Steamship Sailings

TO EUROPE

(All ships sail from New York except as noted otherwise)

Leave New York	SHIP	Ports and Arrival Dates Due Abroad
MARCH		
15	QUEEN ELIZABETH	Cherbourg 3/20; Southampton 3/21
15	JERUSALEM	Madeira 3/22; Gibraltar 3/24; Naples 3/26; Haifa 3/29
16	IVERNIA	Cobh 3/23; Havre, London 3/24
17	PARTHIA	Liverpool 3/25
17	ATLANTIC	Algeciras 3/24; Naples 3/26; Haifa 3/29
17	OLYMPIA	Naples 3/26; Piraeus 3/28; Haifa 3/29; Piraeus 3/31
17	ZION	Gibraltar 3/25; Piraeus 3/29; Haifa 3/31
18	LIBERTE	Plymouth, Havre 3/24
18	NOORDAM	Rotterdam 3/27
18	BREMEN	Cherbourg, Southampton 3/24; Bremerhaven 3/25
21	EMPRESS of ENGLAND	Greenock 3/27; Liverpool 3/28
21¶	NOVA SCOTIA	Liverpool 4/2
22	QUEEN MARY	Cherbourg, Southampton 3/27
22	SYLVANIA	Greenock 3/29; Liverpool 3/30
22	INDEPENDENCE	Algeciras 3/28; Cannes, Genoa 3/30; Naples 3/31
22	RYNDAM	Southampton, Havre 3/31; Rotterdam 4/1
22	EXETER	Cadiz 3/30; Barcelona 4/2; Marseilles 4/3; Naples 4/5; Alexandria 4/8; Beirut 4/10; Piraeus 4/12
23	AMERICA	Cobh 3/29; Havre, Southampton 3/30; Bremenhaven 3/31
23	LEONARDO da VINCI	Gibraltar 3/29; Naples 3/31; Cannes, Genoa 4/1
25‡	LAURENTIA	Glasgow 4/3
27	BERLIN	Southampton 4/5; Bremerhaven 4/7
29	QUEEN ELIZABETH	Cherbourg 4/3; Southampton 4/4
29	SATURNIA	Lisbon 4/5; Gibraltar 4/6; Naples 4/9; Palermo 4/10; Patras 4/11; Dubrovnik 4/12; Venice, Trieste 4/13
30	UNITED STATES	Havre, Southampton 4/4; Bremerhaven 4/5
30	SAXONIA	Cobh 4/6; Havre, Southampton 4/7
31	MEDIA	Bermuda 4/2; Liverpool 4/10
31	STAVANGERFJORD	Kristiansand 4/9; Copenhagen 4/10; Oslo 4/11
APRIL		
1	WESTERDAM	Rotterdam 4/10
4	CRISTOFORO COLOMBO	Gibraltar 4/10; Naples 4/12; Cannes, Genoa 4/13
4¶	NEWFOUNDLAND	Liverpool 4/16
5	QUEEN MARY	Cherbourg, Southampton 4/10
5	LIBERTE	Plymouth, Havre 4/11
5	ISRAEL	Gibraltar 4/13; Piraeus 4/17; Haifa 4/19
7*	EMPRESS of BRITAIN	Greenock 4/13; Liverpool 4/14
7	CARINTHIA	Cobh 4/14; Liverpool 4/15
7	MAASDAM	Cobh 4/15; Southampton, Havre 4/16; Rotterdam 4/17
8	BREMEN	Cherbourg, Southampton 4/14; Bremerhaven 4/15
11	INDEPENDENCE	Algeciras 4/17; Cannes, Genoa 4/19; Naples 4/20
11□	QUEEN FREDERICA	Gibraltar 4/19; Palermo, Naples 4/21; Messina 4/22; Piraeus 4/23
12	QUEEN ELIZABETH	Cherbourg 4/17; Southampton 4/18
12	OSLOFJORD	Bergen 4/19; Stavanger, Kristiansand 4/20; Copenhagen 4/21; Oslo 4/22
13*	IVERNIA	Havre, Southampton 4/20
13	AMERICA	Cobh 4/19; Havre, Southampton 4/20; Bremerhaven 4/21
13*	HOMERIC	Havre, Southampton 4/20; Cuxhaven 4/21
13*	BATORY	Southampton 4/21; Copenhagen 4/23; Gdynia 4/24; Leningrad 4/26
13□	VULCANIA	Ponta Delgada 4/19; Lisbon 4/21; Gibraltar 4/22; Barcelona 4/24; Naples 4/25; Palermo 4/26; Patras 4/27; Dubrovnik 4/28, Venice, Trieste 4/29
14§	RYNDAM	Southampton, Havre 4/22; Rotterdam 4/23
14	NOORDAM	Rotterdam 4/24
14	UNITED STATES	Havre, Southampton 4/19
14	FLANDRE	Southampton 4/20; Havre 4/21
14	EMPRESS of ENGLAND	Greenock 4/20; Liverpool 4/21
14	SYLVANIA	Greenock 4/21; Liverpool 4/22
14	HANSEATIC	Southampton 4/21; Havre 4/22; Cuxhaven 4/23

(Continued on page 42)

(Fares listed on center spread)

* Sails from Montreal. § Sails from Quebec. ¶ Sails from Boston.
□Also sails 1 day later from Boston. ‡ Sails from Saint John, N.B.

Steamship Sailings to Europe (Continued)

Leave New York	SHIP	Ports and Arrival Dates Due Abroad
APRIL		
14	ATLANTIC	Algeciras 4/22; Naples 4/24; Piraeus 4/26; Haifa 4/27
14	OLYMPIA	Lisbon 4/21; Naples, Messina 4/24; Piraeus 4/25; Cyprus, Haifa 4/27; Piraeus 4/29
17	ROTTERDAM	Southampton, Havre 4/24; Rotterdam 4/25
18	LEONARDO da VINCI	Gibraltar 4/24; Naples 4/26; Cannes, Genoa 4/27
19	QUEEN MARY	Cherbourg, Southampton 4/24
19	EXCALIBUR	Cadiz 4/27; Barcelona 4/30; Marseilles 5/1; Naples 5/3; Alexandria 5/6; Beirut 5/8; Piraeus 5/10
21	LIBERTE	Plymouth, Havre 4/27
21	PARTHIA	Liverpool 4/29
22*	SAXONIA	Havre, Southampton 4/29
22	KUNGSHOLM	Bremerhaven 4/30; Copenhagen 5/1; Gothenburg 5/2
22	BERLIN	Southampton 5/1; Bremerhaven 5/3
24	CONSTITUTION	Algeciras 4/30; Cannes, Genoa 5/2; Naples 5/3
24§	IRPINIA	Azores 4/30; Cannes 5/5; Genoa 5/6; Naples 5/7; Palermo 5/8
25¶	NOVA SCOTIA	Liverpool 5/7
26	QUEEN ELIZABETH	Cherbourg 5/1; Southampton 5/2
26	STATENDAM	Southampton, Havre 5/3; Rotterdam 5/4
26	CRISTOFORO COLOMBO	Gibraltar 5/2; Naples 5/4; Cannes, Genoa 5/5
26	STAVANGERFJORD	Kristiansand 5/4; Copenhagen 5/5; Oslo 5/6
27	UNITED STATES	Havre, Southampton 5/2; Bremerhaven 5/3
27	BREMEN	Cherbourg, Southampton 5/3; Bremerhaven 5/4
28*	EMPRESS of BRITAIN	Greenock 5/4; Liverpool 5/5
28*	CARINTHIA	Greenock 5/5; Liverpool 5/6
28	ZION	Madeira 5/5; Gibraltar 5/6; Piraeus 5/10; Haifa 5/12
29	WESTERDAM	Rotterdam 5/8
MAY		
1	INDEPENDENCE	Casablanca 5/7; Algeciras, Gibraltar 5/8; Palermo 5/10; Naples 5/11; Genoa 5/12; Cannes 5/13
2	MAURETANIA	Cobh 5/8; Havre, Southampton 5/9
2	NIEUW AMSTERDAM	Southampton, Havre 5/9; Rotterdam 5/10
2	GRIPSHOLM	Gothenburg 5/10; Helsinki 5/12
3	QUEEN MARY	Cherbourg, Southampton 5/8
3	FLANDRE	Southampton 5/9; Havre 5/10
4	AMERICA	Cobh 5/10; Havre, Southampton 5/11; Bremerhaven 5/12
4	BERGENSFJORD	Kristiansand 5/11; Copenhagen 5/12; Oslo 5/13
4*	ARKADIA	Cobh 5/11; Havre, London 5/12; Amsterdam 5/13; Bremerhaven 5/14
4□	MAASDAM	Galway 5/12; Southampton 5/14; Rotterdam 5/15
4□	SATURNIA	Ponta Delgada 5/10; Lisbon 5/12; Gibraltar 5/13; Barcelona 5/15; Naples 5/16; Palermo 5/17; Patras 5/18; Dubrovnik 5/19; Venice, Trieste 5/20
5	HANSEATIC	Southampton 5/11; Havre 5/12; Cuxhaven 5/13
5*	HOMERIC	Southampton 5/11; Havre 5/12; Cuxhaven 5/13
5*	EMPRESS of CANADA	Greenock 5/11; Liverpool 5/12
5*	IVERNIA	Havre, Southampton 5/12
5	MEDIA	Liverpool 5/13
9	LEONARDO da VINCI	Gibraltar 5/15; Naples 5/17; Cannes, Genoa 5/18
9□	QUEEN FREDERICA	Gibraltar 5/17, Palermo, Naples 5/19; Messina 5/20; Piraeus 5/21
9*	RYNDAM	Southampton, Havre 5/17; Rotterdam 5/18
9¶	NEWFOUNDLAND	Liverpool 5/21
10	QUEEN ELIZABETH	Cherbourg 5/15; Southampton 5/16
10	EXETER	Cadiz 5/18; Barcelona 5/21; Marseilles 5/22; Naples 5/24; Alexandria 5/27; Beirut 5/29; Piraeus 5/31
11	LIBERTE	Plymouth, Havre 5/17
11□	OLYMPIA	Lisbon 5/18; Naples, Messina 5/21; Piraeus 5/22; Cyprus, Haifa 5/24; Piraeus 5/26
12	UNITED STATES	Havre, Southampton 5/17
12*	EMPRESS of ENGLAND	Greenock 5/18; Liverpool 5/19
12*	SAXONIA	Havre, Southampton 5/19
12	SYLVANIA	Cobh 5/19; Liverpool 5/20
13	CONSTITUTION	Casablanca 5/19; Algeciras 5/20; Naples 5/22; Genoa 5/23; Cannes 5/24
13	OSLOFJORD	Bergen 5/20; Stavanger, Kristiansand 5/21; Oslo 5/22

(Continued on page 44)

(Fares listed on center spread)

* Sails from Montreal. ¶ Sails from Boston.
□Also sails 1 day later from Boston. § Sails from Quebec.

SWEDISH AMERICAN LINE

The Swedes had a sterling reputation for both excellent service and very beautiful ships. Although they were perhaps better known as a deluxe, long-distance cruising firm, the Swedish-American liners provided regular two-class service to home waters as well. Sailings were offered between New York and Gothenburg with a call at Copenhagen in each direction.

An alternate Scandinavian service was that of the Norwegian America Line --- with such ships as the STAVANGERFJORD, OSLOFJORD and BERGENSFJORD --- which ran sailings to Oslo, Bergen, Stavanger, Kristiansand and Copenhagen. They turned completely to cruising by the early Seventies.

The **GRIPSHOLM (1957) and the KUNGSHOLM (1966) were the last Swedish-American liners. They had impeccable reputations, both on the Atlantic and in the deluxe cruise trade. The company abandoned its passenger services in 1975 when they could no longer ecomonically maintain their high standards.** [ABOVE] **The two liners meet at the Yokohama Ocean Terminal on March 21st 1973.** [RIGHT] **When the original KUNGHOLM was commissioned in the fall of 1953, she was the first liner on the Atlantic run to feature all outside staterooms**

R. Izawa; Richard Sandstrom Collection.

GRIPSHOLM   Built 1957
Built by: Ansaldo Shipyard,
                Genoa, Italy
23,191 gross tons
631 feet long   82 feet wide
Gotaverken type diesel
Service speed 19 knots
842 passengers
                214 first class;   628 tourist class

KUNGSHOLM   Built 1966
Built by: John Brown & Company Limited,
                Clydebank, Scotland
26,678 gross tons
660 feet long   86 feet wide
Gotaverken diesels geared to twin screw
Service speed 21 knots
750 passengers
                108 first class;   642 tourist class

KUNGSHOLM   Built 1953
Built by: De Schelde Shipyard,
                Flushing, Holland
21,141 gross tons
600 feet long   77 feet wide
B & W - type diesel geared to twin screw
Service speed 19 knots
802 passengers
                176 first class;   626 tourist class

CANADIAN PACIFIC

Steamships were an important part of the enormous Canadian Pacific network of shipping, trains, trucks, telecommunications and even an airline. The famed EMPRESS liners sailed between Liverpool and Greenock in Scotland and then across to Quebec City and Montreal. In winter, during the ice-choked months on the St. Lawrence, the ships went either to Saint John, New Brunswick or to New York for Caribbean cruising. The last of the EMPRESSES, the 27-000-ton EMPRESS OF CANADA of 1961, ended both Canadian Pacific liner operations as well as regular service to Canada in December 1971.

[ABOVE] **The EMPRESS OF SCOTLAND had been the pre-war EMPRESS OF JAPAN. She was the fastest liner on the Pacific sailing between Vancouver and the Orient. After the War and very extensive trooping, she was rerouted to the Atlantic.** [RIGHT] **The EMPRESS OF ENGLAND and her sistership EMPRESS OF BRITAIN were Canadian Pacific's first major liners built after the War.**

Vincent Messina Collection; Canadian Pacific.

EMPRESS OF SCOTLAND   Built 1930
Built by: Fairfield Shipbuilding & Engineering
                Company, Glasgow, Scotland
26,313 gross tons
666 feet long   83 feet wide
Steam turbines geared to twin screw
Service speed 21 knots
708 passengers
                458 first class;   250 tourist class

EMPRESS OF ENGLAND   Built 1957
Built by: Vickers - Armstrong Shipbuilders
                Limited, Newcastle on Tyne, England
25,585 gross tons
640 feet long   85 feet wide
Steam turbines geared to twin screw
Service speed 20 knots
1058 passengers
                160 first class;   898 tourist class

STEFAN BATORY   Built 1952
Built by: Wilton - Fijenoord Shipyard,
          Schiedam, Holland
15,043 gross tons
503 feet long   69 feet wide
Steam turbines geared to single screw
Service speed 16½ knots
773 passengers, one class

QUEEN ELIZABETH 2   Built 1969
Built by: Upper Clyde Shipbuilders
         Limited, Clydebank, Scotland
65,863 gross tons
963 feet long   105 feet wide
Steam turbines geared to twin screw
Service speed 28½ knots
2005 passengers
        564 first class;   1441 tourist class

THE LAST ATLANTIC LINERS

The last Atlantic liners by the early Eighties were Cunard's QUEEN ELIZABETH 2 and the STEFAN BATORY of the Polish Ocean Lines. Although both ships spend about half their year in cruising, the crossings made mostly in the summer months are supported by loyalists to the earlier age of the transatlantic liners. The modern QUEEN aptly carries the colors of the distinguished Cunard name, which has been so much a part of the history of the North Atlantic. The STEFAN BATORY --- being considerably older, smaller, slower and less famous --- is assuredly the last of a type of passenger vessel that was once so common place to the Atlantic sealanes.

[TOP] **The STEFAN BATORY docks at Gdynia.** [UPPER LEFT] **The QUEEN ELIZABETH 2 sails from Southampton.**

Polish Ocean Lines; J.K. Byass.

26

CHAPTER TWO:
LATIN AMERICA

ELMA LINES

The ARGENTINA of 1949 was a strikingly handsome example of a combination passenger-cargo liner.

Roger Sherlock

Argentina was alone among the South American countries to be involved in deep-sea passenger trading, although never with very large or powerful ships. Instead, operations were limited to either all-first class combination passenger ships or high-capacity immigrant carriers. For the ELMA Lines (Empresas Lineas Maritimas Argentinas), a combo trio --- the ARGENTINA, LIBERTAD and URUGUAY --- worked the trade between Buenos Aires, Montevideo, Santos and Rio de Janeiro to Lisbon, Le Havre and London. Another trio --- the RIO DE LA PLATA, RIO JACHAL and RIO TUNUYAN --- sailed to New York. The immigrant runs included the sisters ALBERTO DODERO and YAPEYU to Amsterdam and Hamburg, and the CORRIENTES and SALTA to Genoa, Naples, Vigo and Lisbon.

ARGENTINA   Built 1949
Built by: Vickers - Armstrong Limited,
           Barrow - in - Furness, England
12,459 gross tons
530 feet long   27 feet wide
Steam turbines geared to twin screw
Service speed 18 knots
74 first class passengers only

ITALIAN LINE

The state-owned Italian Line had an alternate yet equally profitable service to their fancy New York operations. Between Naples, Genoa and Cannes out to Rio, Santos, Montevideo and Buenos Aires, the Company ran the pre-war CONTE BIANCAMANO and CONTE GRANDE and the newer sisters AUGUSTUS and GIULIO CESARE, all of which carried three classes. First class was said to be for rich Europeans and Latin Americans, and the high Catholic clergy. Cabin class was more for tourists and the lower clergy. Tourist or third class was for immigrants, often sailing in both directions, seeking resettlement and a new life.

Further Italian Line passenger service was offered to the West Coast of South America --- to Buenaventura in Colombia, Callao in Peru and Antofagasta and Valparaiso in Chile, all via the Caribbean and Panama.

[ABOVE] **The AUGUSTUS and her twin sistership the GIULIO CESARE were among the biggest motorliners ever built.** [UPPER RIGHT] **The CONTE BIANCAMANO and her near sister the CONTE GRANDE were two of the four largest Italian liners to survive the Second World War. After thorough conversions that included greatly altered interior accommodations, the pair saw much further profitable service. The BIANCAMANO had the added benefit of sailing to South America in the winter and then to New York in the summers for the height of the tourist season. [RIGHT] Lloyd Triestino's AUSTRALIA, NEPTUNIA and OCEANIA were taken over by the Italian Line in 1963 and renamed the DONIZETTI, ROSSINI and VERDI. "The Three Musicians" were used for the West Coast of South America Service.**

Three photos: Roger Sherlock.

CONTE BIANCAMANO   Built 1925
Built by: William Beardmore & Company,
                    Glasgow, Scotland
23,842 gross tons
665 feet long   76 feet wide
Steam turbines geared to twin screw
Service speed 18 knots
1578 passengers
                215 first class;   333 cabin class
                1030 tourist class

AUGUSTUS   Built 1952
Built by: Cantieri Riuniti dell 'Adriatico
                    Trieste, Italy
27,090 gross tons
680 feet long   87 feet wide
Fiat diesels geared to twin screw
Service speed 21 knots
1182 passengers
              180 first class;   288 cabin class
              714 tourist class

ROSSINI   Built 1951
Built by: Cantieri Riuniti dell 'Adriatico,
                    Trieste, Italy
13,225 gross tons
528 feet long   69 feet wide
Sulzer diesels geared to twin screw
Service speed 18 knots
600 passengers
              160 first class;   440 tourist class

BOOTH LINE
PACIFIC STEAM NAVIGATION
FYFFES LINE

Until the mid-Sixties, Britain still had the most extensive passenger ship network in the world. One of her more unusual services was the Booth Line passenger-cargo run to the Amazon. Ships such as the HUBERT and ANSELM sailed from Liverpool via Lisbon and Madeira and then to Barbados and Trinidad, to Belem and finally along the Amazon to Manaus.

Pacific Steam Navigation offered "big ship" service to the Caribbean and West Coast of South America. The REINA DEL MAR sailed from Liverpool to Bermuda, Nassau, Havana, Kingston, La Guaira, Curacao, Cartagena, then through the Panama Canal to Callao, Antofagasta and Valparaiso, before reversing course and heading home.

The passenger-carrying "banana boats" of the Fyffes Line offered yet another tropic service --- from Southampton to Barbados, Trinidad, Jamaica and Bermuda.

GOLFITO   Built 1949
Built by: Alexander Stephen & Sons Limited,
               Glasgow, Scotland
8,740 gross tons
447 feet long   62 feet wide
Steam turbines geared to twin screw
Service speed 17½ knots
111 first class passengers only

[RIGHT] **The combination liners GOLFITO and her near sister-ship, the CAMITO, were the last "banana boats" to carry more than the customary 12 passengers. Both were extremely popular and comfortable. In her memoirs, the late Princess Alice wrote, "One of the highlights of my winter is a voyage in one of the Fyffes boats— preferably the GOLFITO or CAMITO."**

Alex Duncan.

[LEFT] **Booth Line's ANSELM traded on the extensive Liverpool-Amazon run. She was acquired in 1961 from the Belgian Line. Originally BAUDOUINVILLE, and later the THYSVILLE, she was used on their Congo service. Two years later she was sold to the Blue Star Line becoming the IBERIA STAR. She later sailed as the AUSTRALASIA for the Austasia Line of Singapore.**

Alex Duncan.

ANSELM   Built 1950
Built by: John Cockerill S. A.,
           Hoboken, Belgium
10,950 gross tons
505 feet long   65 feet wide
B & W diesels geared to single screw
Service speed 16 knots
228 passengers
        128 first class;   100 tourist class

[RIGHT] **The Pacific Steam Navigation's REINA DEL MAR—"The Queen of the Sea"—was one of the last examples of a three-class passenger liner. In the early Sixties, as her Latin American sailings waned, she turned to a new, highly profitable life as a cruise ship for Union-Castle.**

Roger Sherlock.

REINA DEL MAR   Built 1956
Built by: Harland & Wolf Limited,
          Belfast, Northern Ireland
20,234 gross tons
601 feet long   78 feet wide
Steam turbines geared to twin screw
Service speed 18 knots
766 passengers
        207 first class;   216 cabin class
        343 tourist class

FRENCH LINE
CHARGEURS REUNIS
ROYAL NETHERLANDS STEAMSHIP CO.

The French and Dutch --- like the British --- had strong reason for passenger service to the Caribbean. Colonial outposts prompted a constant relay of government ministers and their entourages, families, civil servants, technicians and workers, and even police and military forces on occasion.

The French Line's ANTILLES --- along with older COLOMBIE and then the FLANDRE on occasion --- sailed to Guadeloupe and Martinique as well as several other Caribbean islands. The combo liners of the Royal Netherlands Steamship Company ---

KNSM as it was sometimes more briefly known --- ran services out to Dutch Guiana as well as Curacao and Aruba. Added service calls were made at Barbados, Trinidad, Jamaica, Cuba and Haiti. These more extensive tropical services were also quite ideal for roundtrip holiday voyages of, say, a month or longer.

Although not with the same political reasoning, the French --- namely the Chargeurs Reunis and Compagnie Sud-Atlantique --- ran an established service from Le Havre (and also Hamburg and Antwerp) out to Rio, Santos, Montevideo and Buenos Aires.

LOUIS LUMIERE   Built 1952
Built by: Chantiers et Ateliers de St. Nazaire,
                Penhoet, France
12,358 gross tons
537 feet long   64 feet wide
Sulzer diesels geared to twin screw
Service speed 16 knots
436 passengers
            110 first class;   326 third class

[RIGHT] **The combination liners of the Chargeurs Reunis—such as the LOUIS LUMIERE—were later taken over by Messageries Maritimes, in a coordinated worldwide French passenger ship reorganization.**

Messageries Maritimes.

[LEFT] **The PRINS DER NEDERLANDEN and her sistership, the ORANJE NASSAU, were the biggest post-war passenger ships to be built for the very large Royal Netherlands Steamship Company. In the early Seventies, as the Caribbean liner trade declined, these ships were sold to the Cuban Government for use as transports and training ships.**

Alex Duncan.

PRINS DER NEDERLANDEN   Built 1957
Built by: P. Smit, Jr. Shipyard,
                    Rotterdam, Holland
7,220 gross tons
432 feet long   57 feet wide
B & W diesel geared to single screw
Service speed 15½ knots
184 passengers, one class only

[ABOVE] **The French Line's ANTILLES was nearly identical to the transatlantic FLANDRE. One quite noticeable difference was that the former ship's funnel was higher. Sadly, the ANTILLES was wrecked off Mustique in January 1971, following a fatal fire. Her remains can be seen to this day.**

Roger Sherlock.

ANTILLES   Built 1952
Built by: Naval Dockyard,
                    Brest, France
19,828 gross tons
599 feet long   80 feet wide
Steam turbines geared to twin screw
Service speed 22 knots
778 passengers
            404 first class;   285 cabin class
            89 tourist class

HAMBURG - SOUTH AMERICAN LINE

The Hamburg-South American Line had a particularly large liner fleet before the Second World War, but opted to resume passenger service only with combination ships. However, the standard on these ships was nothing if not exceptionally deluxe, catering only to a first class trade.

Ships such as the SANTAS ELENA, INES, ISABEL, TERESA and URSULA (not to be confused with some of the American-flag Grace liners, which also used a SANTA naming theme) sailed between Hamburg, Bremen and Rotterdam out to Rio, Santos, Montevideo and Buenos Aires. Other occasional intermediate calls included Las Palmas in the Canaries and Recife, Salvador and Ilheos in Brazil.

SANTA ISABEL   Built 1951
Built by: Howaldtswerke Shipyard,
                  Hamburg, Germany
6,982 gross tons
479 feet long   61 feet wide
M.A.N. type diesel geared to single screw
Service speed 13 knots
28 first class passengers

[ABOVE] The SANTA ISABEL was one of six combination ships with which the famed Hamburg-South American Line reopened its post-war passenger service to the East Coast of South America. The charm and elegance of the ships were captured [UPPER RIGHT] in the Lounge-Bar and [RIGHT] in a deluxe single.

This page: Roger Sherlock.
Opposite: Hamburg-South American Line.

COSTA LINE
GRIMALDI - SIOSA LINES

The Costa Line of Genoa --- which has the largest cruiseship operation apart from the Soviets at the time of writing [1983] --- began passenger service in 1948 with the ANNA C., on the immigrant run to Brazil, Uruguay and Argentina. Continued success followed, prompting newer and larger ships. The stark, austere immigrant quarters later gave way to a more comfortable tourist class.

The Grimaldi-Siosa Lines --- another family-owned Italian firm --- also traded on the South American immigrant run, using such ships as the VENEZUELA, profitably sailing in her third life. The Company's IRPINIA earned double profits for many years. Outwards, to the Caribbean and Venezuela, she sailed with Spanish immigrants. Then, homebound, she carried tens of thousands of Jamaicans to Britain.

ANNA C.   Built 1929
Built by: Lithgows Limited,
             Glasgow, Scotland
11,736 gross tons
524 feet long   65 feet wide
Fiat diesels geared to twin screw
Service speed 18 knots
1001 passengers
         337 first class;   664 third class

[ABOVE] **Costa Line's first passenger ship, the ANNA C., was placed on the Italy-South American run in March 1948. She had previously been the SOUTHERN PRINCE for the Furness-Prince Line.**

V.H. Young.

[ABOVE] **The IRPINIA was the first major passenger ship to be owned by Grimaldi-Siosa. Originally, she was of two-funnel design. Her early years were spent as the CAMPANA for the French, on both the Far Eastern and South American runs. In 1979, she reached her fiftieth year, a distinction given to very few passenger ships. Soon thereafter she went to the breakers after a long and profitable life.** [BELOW] **Siosa's VENEZUELA had been the DE GRASSE for the French Line. She served on both North Atlantic and West Indies routes. In 1953, she went to Canadian Pacific as their EMPRESS OF AUSTRALIA. In 1962 she was grounded near Cannes and found to be beyond repair and subsequently junked.**

Roger Sherlock; Roger Scozzafava.

VENEZUELA   Built 1924
Built by: Cammell Laird & Company
                   Birkenhead, England
18,567 gross tons
574 feet long   71 feet wide
Steam turbines geared to twin screw
Service speed 16 knots
1480 passengers
           180 first class;   500 tourist class;
           800 third class

IRPINIA   Built 1929
Built by: Swan, Hunter & Wigham Richardson
                   Limited, Newcastle, England
13,204 gross tons
537 feet long   67 feet wide
Steam turbines geared to twin screw
Service speed 16 knots
1181 passengers
           209 first class;   972 tourist class

SPANISH LINE
YBARRA LINE

The state-owned Spanish Line (the Compania Transatlantica Espanola) maintained three passenger services: an immigrant run from Spain to Venezuela and the Caribbean (and then returning with West Indians to England); a three-class service from Italy and Spain to the Caribbean and Mexico; and a two-class run from Spanish ports to New York, Cuba, Puerto Rico and Mexico.

The Ybarra Line so designed their two largest (and last) liners --- the CABO SAN ROQUE and CABO SAN VINCENTE --- to sail for part of the year with both first class and immigrant traffic to the East Coast of South America from Italy and Spain, and then for the remainder on summer cruises, mostly from Spanish ports.

CABO SAN ROQUE   Built 1957
Built by: Societa Espanola de Construction
            Naval, Bilbao, Spain
14,491 gross tons
557 feet long   69 feet wide
Sulzer diesels geared to twin screw
Service speed 20 knots
823 passengers
            241 first class;   582 tourist class

[ABOVE] **The twin sisters CABO SAN ROQUE and CABO SAN VICENTE were the largest passenger liners ever built in Spanish yards. Although designed primarily for Latin American liner service; both made extensive cruises— particularly during the peak holiday months of July and August.**

Michael D.J. Lennon.

MONTSERRAT   Built 1945
Built by: California Shipbuilding Corporation,
           Los Angeles, California, USA
9,001 gross tons
455 feet long   62 feet wide
Steam turbines geared to single screw
Service speed 16 knots
708 tourist class passengers

[ABOVE] **The Spanish Line's MONTSERRAT and her near—sister, the BEGONA, were especially redesigned for low-fare passenger service. Both had been originally American— built Victory ships, freighters with wartime troop accomodation. As passenger vessels for the Spanish, they earned double profits on their Atlantic voyages to and from the Caribbean. Westbound, they carried Spanish immigrants, bound for resettlement in Venezuela. Eastward, they transported Jamaicans mostly to Britain.** [BELOW] **The sisters SATRUSTEGUI and VIRGINIA DE CHURRUCA handled the Spanish Line's Caribbean trade out of Italian and home ports.**

Both photos: Roger Sherlock.

SATRUSTEGUI   Built 1948
Built by: Union Naval de Levante,
           Valencia, Spain
6,518 gross tons
401 feet long   55 feet wide
B & W-type diesel geared to twin screw
Service speed 15½ knots
201 passengers
          65 first class;   54 Cabin class
          82 tourist class

ROYAL MAIL LINES

Britain's Royal Mail Lines had a long tradition of service to eastern South America. The flagship ANDES was particularly popular with roundtrip, holiday passengers, who enjoyed the full voyage to Rio, Santos, Montevideo and Buenos Aires from Southampton. The "Highland class" sisters --- the HIGHLAND BRIGADE, HIGHLAND CHIEFTAIN, HIGHLAND MONARCH and HIGHLAND PRINCESS, and then later three newer units named AMAZON, ARAGON and ARLANZA --- maintained a paced service out of London but with sizeable revenues coming from cargo as well, particularly the northbound beef from the Argentine.

A shift in both the passenger and freight business prompted Royal Mail to withdraw from the South American liner service in 1969.

[ABOVE] **The ANDES was the last flagship for the Royal Mail Lines, a part of the large Furness Withy Group. After being withdrawn from South American service in 1959, she turned exclusively to luxury cruising, for which she established a very high reputation with the British travelling public. Cruise voyages in the ANDES, with her club-like tone, were often thought to be akin to an exclusive fraternity. Many travelers came year after year— on the same voyages, in the same cabins, with the same stewards and waiters.**

British Railways, Southern Region.

ANDES Built 1939
Built by: Harland & Wolff Limited,
    Belfast, Northern Ireland
25,676 gross tons
669 feet long   83 feet wide
Steam turbines geared to twin screw
Service speed 21 knots
528 passengers
            324 first class;   204 second class

HIGHLAND BRIGADE   Built 1930
Built by: Harland & Wolff Limited,
               Belfast, Northern Ireland
14,216 gross tons
544 feet long   69 feet wide
B & W -type diesels geared to twin screw
Service speed 15 knots
450 passengers
               100 first class;   350 third class

ALCANTARA   Built 1926
Built by: Harland & Wolff Limited,
               Belfast, Northern Ireland
22,607 gross tons
667 feet long   78 feet wide
Steam turbines geared to twin screw
Service speed 18 knots
860 passengers
               220 first class;   180 second class
               460 third class

[ABOVE] **Royal Mail's four Highland sisters — including the HIGHLAND BRIGADE — had the rather stumped-look of motorships built in the late Twenties and early Thirties. In addition to providing regular passenger sailings from the Port of London, they drew great profits in the homebound meat trade from the Argentine.**
[LOWER LEFT] **The ALCANTARA, also for Royal Mail, assisted the larger ANDES on the express run between Southampton and the East Coast of South America. Near the end of her commercial life, in 1958, she was used by film crews for deck scenes in the making of ''A Night To Remember,'' the story of the TITANIC tragedy.**

Royal Mail Lines; World Ship Society Collection.

MOORE McCORMACK LINES
GRACE LINE

Prominently carrying the Stars and Stripes to Latin America were the Moore-McCormack and Grace lines, both of New York. "Mor-Mac" offered 33-day roundtrips as far as Buenos Aires and return. It's original "Good Neighbor" trio --- the ARGENTINA, BRAZIL and URUGUAY of 1928-29 --- later gave way to the new ARGENTINA and BRASIL of 1958. They terminated their liner runs in 1969. Later, they became the VEENDAM and VOLENDAM for Holland-America Cruises.

Grace had a sizeable fleet of combination ships, all of which made rich profits as cargo carriers. Only first class passenger space was offered, generally of extremely high standard. The flagships SANTA PAULA and SANTA ROSA --- which replaced an earlier pair of the same names in 1958 --- traded on the 13-day service out of New York to Curacao, LaGuaira, Aruba, Kingston, Nassau and Port Everglades, Florida. The nine sister-ships of the 52-passenger SANTA SOFIA class went further and longer into the Caribbean, sailing up to 18- and 24-days and including such ports as Santo Domingo, Cartagena, Santa Marta, Barranquilla and Maracaibo. For the West Coast run to South America, Grace added four early-design container-passenger types --- the SANTAS MAGDALENA, MARIA, MARIANA and MERCEDES --- that sailed via Panama to Buenaventura in Colombia, Guayaquil in Ecuador and Callao in Peru. Grace ended its passenger service in 1971 and subsequently sold all of its ships.

[ABOVE] **The URUGUAY—outbound and passing the famed Woolworth Building in Lower Manhattan— was part of Mor-Mac's "Good Neighbor" trio. However, she was the first to be retired (in 1954) and spent many years in reserve before being scrapped in the mid-Sixties.**

Steamship Historical Society of America.

URUGUAY   Built 1929
Built by: Newport News Shipbuilding &
           Drydock Co.,
           Newport News, Virginia, USA
20,237 gross tons
601 feet long   80 feet wide
Steam turbo-electric geared to twin screw
Service speed 18 knots
510 passengers
           350 first class;   160 cabin class

[ABOVE] **Grace Line's SANTA ROSA and her sistership, the SANTA PAULA, were very fine liners, designed especially for the Caribbean trade. Both had balanced provision for high-standard, first class passengers and cargo. After ending their passenger days in 1971, the PAULA went on to become a permanently moored hotel in Kuwait while the ROSA has never been reactivated. At the time of writing (1983), she remains in very poor neglected condition in the backwaters of Baltimore.** [BELOW] **The SANTA MARIANA and her three sisters—the SANTAS MARIA, MAGDALENA and MERCEDES— were especially designed for the West Coast of South America run and, in a pre-containership era, carried their own container gantry cranes onboard. In later years, the stovepipe exhaust was replaced by a funnel, lifted aboard at dockside by a helicopter.**

Both photos: Grace Line.

SANTA ROSA   Built 1958
Built by: Newport News Shipbuilding &
                 Drydock Co.,
                 Newport News, Virginia, USA
15,366 gross tons
584 feet long   84 feet wide
Steam turbines geared to twin screw
Service speed 20 knots
300 first class passengers

SANTA MARIANA   Built 1963
Built by: Bethlehem Steel Company,
                 Sparrows Point, Maryland, USA
14,442 gross tons
547 feet long   79 feet wide
Steam turbines geared to single screw
Service speed 20 knots
125 first class passengers

Grace "Santas" provide
ALL OUTSIDE ROOMS, EACH WITH PRIVATE FRESH WATER BATH

TELEPHONE IN EVERY ROOM

OUTDOOR TILED SWIMMING POOLS

BEACH DECKS

OPEN AIR DINING ROOMS ON PROMENADE DECKS

SPACIOUS LIVING ROOMS

CLUB BARS

DANCE ORCHESTRAS

DOROTHY GRAY BEAUTY SALONS

PRE-RELEASE TALKIES

RADIO PROGRAMS

DECK SPORTS — GYMNASIUMS

PALM COURTS — LIBRARIES

LAUNDRIES — BARBER SHOPS

NOVELTY SHOPS

MECHANICAL VENTILATION

PHOTO DARKROOMS

CHAPTER THREE:
SOUTH TO AFRICA

UNION - CASTLE LINE

[LEFT] A dramatic aerial view of South-ampton's Western Docks during the de-vastating British Maritime Strike of May-June 1966. In the foreground, moored three abreast, is a trio of Union Castle ships: GOOD HOPE CASTLE, REINA DEL MAR and EDINBURGH CASTLE. Just beyond are P&O's ARCADIA and CANBERRA. Futher along are the S.A. VAAL, QUEEN ELIZABETH and — most distantly— the WINDSOR CASTLE in the King George V Graving Dock.

Union-Castle Line.

[ABOVE] The TRANSVAAL CASTLE of 1962 was the last passenger liner to be built for the once mighty Union-Castle fleet. She is shown berthed along the Southampton Docks, just prior to her maiden voyage, with the older ATHLONE CASTLE in the background.

British Transport Commission.

Britain's Union-Castle Mail Steamship Company Limited was by far the best known and most historic passenger ship firm sailing to Africa. Steeped in tradition, it was often said that one could set a clock by the precision Thursday afternoon sailings from Southampton of the Castle mailships bound for the South African Cape.

Union-Castle first class accommodations offered extremely high standard, hotel-like quarters --- most agreeable to the British tourists who used them for extended South African holidays. The tourist class sections were more for new settlers, students and budget tourists. At one of its peaks, in 1960, there were thirteen Castle liners in service: the brand new flagship WINDSOR CASTLE, the PENDENNIS CASTLE, the sisters EDINBURGH and PRETORIA CASTLE, the CAPETOWN

TRANSVAAL CASTLE   Built 1962
Built by: John Brown & Company Ltd.,
                    Clydebank, Scotland
32.697 gross tons
760 feet long   90 feet wide
Steam turbines geared to twin screw
Service speed 22 knots
736 hotel class passengers

CASTLE, the sisterships ATHLONE and STIRLING CAS-
TLE, and the CARNARVON CASTLE, all of which were on
the express Cape mail service, and then the RHODESIA,
KENYA, BRAEMAR, DURBAN and WARWICK CASTLES
on the Round Africa service. In addition to their two-class
passenger quarters, all of these ships had quite large cargo
capacities.

The mail run sailed out of Southampton via Las Palmas
and/or Madeira to Capetown, Port Elizabeth, East London and
Durban, before reversing for home. The Round Africa ships
sailed from both London and Rotterdam and went out via Las
Palmas, Ascension, St. Helena, Walvis Bay, Capetown, Port
Elizabeth, Durban and then homeward via Lourenco Marques,
Beira, Dar-es-Salaam, Zanzibar, Tanga, Mombasa, Aden,
Suez, Port Said, Genoa, Marseilles and Gibraltar. Also, the
Round Africa liners sailed on a reverse pattern --- out via the
Mediterranean and East Africa, and home via the Atlantic.

Union-Castle passenger services gradually declined untill
1977, when the last liners, the WINDSOR CASTLE and S.A.
VAAL (the former TRANSVAAL CASTLE), made the final
runs. In passenger ships anals, this was the last major operation that remained a full liner service to the end, undaunted by
the lures of even parttime cruising. Along with jet competition, the transition to containerized freight shipping prompted
this particular demise.

Modern stylings on the historic South African mail run: [ABOVE] **The Vineyard Bar and** [BELOW] **the Restaurant aboard the TRANSVAAL CASTLE of 1962.**

Union-Castle Line.

[LEFT]   Most of the older Union-Castle liners had a very distinguishable profile: a long, low superstructure, two tall masts, a casual rake and wide, flat-topped red-and-black funnels. The CARNARVON CASTLE was among the eldest in the post-war fleet and served until 1962.

F. W. Hawks.

CARNARVON CASTLE   Built 1926
Built by: Harland & Wolff Limited
               Belfast, Northern Ireland
20,148 gross tons
686 feet long   73 feet wide
B & W-type diesel geared to twin screw
Service speed 20 knots
584 passengers
               134 first class;   450 tourist class

ELDER DEMPSTER LINE
BELGIAN LINE

Colonial links in Africa were, of course, strong reasoning for combination passenger-cargo services. The Elder Dempster Lines of Liverpool sent its ships, including their flagship AUREOL, out to British dominated West Africa, to such ports as Freetown, Takoradi and Lagos.

The Belgian Line --- the Compagnie Maritime Belge --- had seven combo liners (the BAUDOUINVILLE, JADOTVILLE, ALBERTVILLE, ELISABETHVILLE, LEOPOLDVILLE, THYSVILLE and CHARLESVILLE) on the Congo run, out from Antwerp to the ports of Lobito, Matadi and Boma. Rather uniquely, even despite the political changes, this service continues at the time of writing, although with two newer combo liners, the 71-passenger FABIOLAVILLE and KANANGA. The latter flies the flag of Zaire.

[ABOVE] **The AUREOL was the flagship of the Elder Dempster fleet. In addition to one-way trade, she often took passengers on roundtrip cruise-like voyages to West African ports. Retired in 1974, she now serves as an accomodation ship in Saudi Arabia.**

Roger Sherlock.

AUREOL   Built 1951
Built by: Alexander Stephen & Sons Ltd.,
                    Glasgow, Scotland
14,038 gross tons
537 feet long   70 feet wide
Doxford type diesels geared to twin screw
Service speed 16 knots
395 passengers
            295 first class;   76 cabin class
            24 interchangeable

LEOPOLDVILLE   Built 1948
Built by: John Cockerill S.A.,
                  Hoboken, Belgium
10,877 gross tons
505 feet long   65 feet wide
B & W-type diesels geared to single screw
Service speed 16½ knots
207 one-class passengers

The LEOPOLDVILLE was one of five sisterships on the Belgian Line's Congo service.

Belgian Line.

WORLD'S LONGEST PASSENGER SHIPS —1967

Length	Tonnage	Ship/Company
1035'	66.348	FRANCE [CGT]
1031'	83.673	QUEEN ELIZABETH [Cunard]
1018'	81.237	QUEEN MARY [Cunard]
990'	52.072	UNITED STATES [US Lines]
963'	58.000	Unnamed [Cunard] [Queen Elizabeth 2]
902'	45.911	MICHELANGELO [Italian]
902'	45.911	RAFFAELLO [Italian]
818'	45.733	CANBERRA [P&O]
804'	41.915	ORIANA [P&O]
783'	37.640	WINDSOR CASTLE [U'Castle]
774'	39.241	OCEANIC [Home Lines]
763'	28.582	PENDENNIS CASTLE [U'Castle]
761'	33.340	LEONARDO DA VINCI [Italian]
760'	32.697	S. A. VAAL [Safmarine]
758'	36.982	NIEUW AMSTERDAM [Holl-Amer]
748'	38.645	ROTTERDAM [Holl-Amer]
747'	28.629	S. A. ORANJE [Safmarine]
747'	28.625	EDINBURGH CASTLE [U'Castle]
734'	27.002	CAPETOWN CASTLE [U'Castle]
723'	34.449	AUSTRALIS [Chandris]
723'	28.790	ORSOVA [P&O]
721'	29.734	ARCADIA [P&O]
719'	29.614	IBERIA [P&O]
715'	34.172	CARONIA [Cunard]
712'	30.567	EUGENIO C. [Costa]
709'	28.396	ORCADES [P&O]
709'	27.955	HIMALAYA [P&O]
709'	27.632	ORONSAY [P&O]
702'	27.907	GALILEO GALILEI [Triestino]
702'	27.905	GUGLIELMO MARCONI [Triestino]
700'	29.429	CRISTOFORO COLOMBO [Italian]
697'	32.336	BREMEN [North German Lloyd]
683'	30.293	CONSTITUTION [Amer Export]
683'	30.293	INDEPENDENCE [Amer Export]
681'	27.078	GIULIO CESARE [Italian]
680'	27.090	AUGUSTUS [Italian]
676'	23.500	SOVETSKY SOJUS [USSR]
672'	24.261	CHUSAN [P&O]
669'	26.435	ANDES [Royal Mail]
665'	23.580	HENRIETTA LATSI [Latsis]
664'	23.732	MARIANNA LATSI [Latsis]
661'	26.678	KUNGSHOLM [Swed-Amer]
656'	24.377	ANGELINA LAURO [Lauro]
650'	27.284	EMPRESS OF CANADA [Can Pacific]
650'	24.731	NORTHERN STAR [Shaw Savill]
642'	24.294	STATENDAM [Holl-Amer]
642'	23.306	INFANTE DOM HENRIQUE [Colonial]
642'	24.351	ELLINIS [Chandris]
640'	26.254	QUEEN ANNA MARIA [Greek Line]
640'	25.585	EMPRESS OF ENGLAND [Can Pacific]
638'	24.907	HOMERIC [Home Lines]
634'	19.116	SAFINA-E-HUJJAJ [Pan Islamic]
631'	23.629	ACHILLE LAURO [Lauro]
631'	23.191	GRIPSHOLM [Swed-Amer]
631'	18.655	LURLINE [Matson]
630'	23.970	CARIBIA [Siosa]

Length	Tonnage	Ship/Owner
629'	25.320	SHALOM [Zim]
625'	19.393	PRINCIPE PERFEITO [Nacional]
623'	18.920	PRESIDENT ROOSEVELT [Amer President]
617'	20.664	ARGENTINA [Moore McCormack]
617'	20.664	BRASIL [Moore McCormack]
615'	24.002	SAGAFJORD [Norw-Amer]
611'	22.640	OLYMPIA [Greek Line]
610'	21.765	VERA CRUZ [Colonial]
609'	23.764	FAIRSTAR [Sitmar]
609'	21.867	RANGITANE [NZ Shipping]
609'	21.809	RANGITOTO [NZ Shipping]
609'	20.906	SANTA MARIA [Colonial]
609'	20.527	NEVASA [British India]
609'	19.339	PRESIDENT CLEVELAND [Amer President]
609'	19.339	PRESIDENT WILSON [Amer President]
608'	22.637	FRANCONIA [Cunard]
608'	22.592	CARMANIA [Cunard]
608'	21.989	SYLVANIA [Cunard]
608'	21.947	CARINTHIA [Cunard]
606'	20.416	FEDERICO C. [Costa]
604'	20.204	SOUTHERN CROSS [Shaw Savill]
601'	21.501	REINA DEL MAR [Union-Castle]
600'	21.164	EUROPA [North German Lloyd]
600'	20.477	FLANDRE [CGT]
599'	19.828	ANTILLES [CGT]
595'	18.400	PATRIS [Chandris]
595'	15.585	SAVANNAH [US Govt]
584'	20.368	AMAZON [Royal Mail]
584'	20.362	ARAGON [Royal Mail]
584'	20.362	ARLANZA [Royal Mail]
584'	17.851	RUAHINE [NZ Shipping]
584'	17.870	ROSSIA [USSR]
584'	15.371	SANTA ROSA [Grace]
584'	15.371	SANTA PAULA [Grace]
584'	13.694	RANDFONTEIN [Holl-Africa]
582'	21.329	QUEEN FREDERICA [Chandris]
580'	17.986	PASTEUR [Mess Maritimes]
579'	15.719	ENRICO C. [Costa]
578'	19.861	IVAN FRANKO [USSR]
578'	19.861	ALEXANDR PUSHKIN [USSR]
578'	19.861	TARAS SHEVCHENKO [USSR]
578'	18.739	BERGENSFJORD [Norw-Amer]
577'	17.891	GUNUNG DJATI [Pelni]
577'	16.844	OSLOFJORD [Norw-Amer]
576'	17.042	KENYA CASTLE [Union Castle]
576'	17.038	RHODESIA CASTLE [Union Castle]
573'	14.917	VICTORIA [Incres]
564'	14.136	ATLANTIC [Amer Export]
563'	14.812	MARIPOSA [Matson]
563'	14.799	MONTEREY [Matson]
561'	15.911	GOTHIC [Shaw Savill]
561'	15.896	CERAMIC [Shaw Savill]
559'	14.304	RUYS [Royal Interocean]
559'	14.300	TEGELBERG [Royal Interocean]
559'	14.285	BOISSEVAIN [Royal Interocean]
558'	13.821	CHITRAL [P&O]

WORLD'S LONGEST PASSENGER SHIPS — 1967

Length	Tonnage	Ship/Owner	Length	Tonnage	Ship/Owner
558'	13.809	CATHAY [P&O]	527'	12.460	JEAN MERMOZ [Cie Paquetbots]
556'	15.465	FLAVIA [Cogedar]	527'	10.549	ORANJEFONTEIN [Holl-Africa]
556'	14.569	CABO SAN VICENTE [Ybarra]	526'	14.287	BATORY [Gdynia Amer]
556'	14.491	CABO SAN ROQUE [Ybarra]	525'	12.387	VOLKERFREUNDSCHAFT [E,German]
551'	14.224	ANCERVILLE [Paquet]	524'	12.055	RUSS [USSR]
550'	13.078	ANGOLA [Nacional]	524'	12.049	ILLICH [USSR]
550'	12.976	MOCAMBIQUE [Nacional]	524'	12.030	ANNA C. [Costa]
550'	11.347	RIO TUNUYAN [ELMA Lines]	523'	11.540	YAPEYU [ELMA Lines]
550'	11.317	RIO JACHAL [ELMA Lines]	523'	11.521	ALBERTO DODERO [ELMA Lines]
549'	12.712	CALEDONIEN [Mess Maritimes]	523'	11.434	AFRICA [Triestino]
549'	12.614	TAHITIEN [Mess Maritimes]	522'	11.879	AUSONIA [Adriatica]
547'	14.442	SANTA MAGDALENA [Grace]	522'	11.695	VICTORIA [Triestino]
547'	14.442	SANTA MARIA [Grace]	522'	11.693	ASIA [Triestino]
547'	14.442	SANTA MARIANA [Grace]	522'	11.440	EUROPA [Triestino]
547'	14.442	SANTA MERCEDES [Grace]	517'	12.796	DEVONIA [Br India]
541'	13.363	CITY OF PORT ELIZABETH [Ellerman]	517'	12.620	DUNERA [Br India]
541'	13.345	CITY OF DURBAN [Ellerman]	517'	12.598	KUALA LUMPUR [China Nav]
541'	13.345	CITY OF EXETER [Ellerman]	516'	13.851	OCEAN MONARCH [Furness]
541'	13.345	CITY OF YORK [Ellerman]	513'	10.864	ARGENTINA MARU [Mitsui-OSK]
540'	14.464	KENYA [British India]	512'	12.628	SAKURA MARU [Mitsui-OSK]
540'	14.430	UGANDA [British India]	511'	10.100	BRAZIL MARU [Mitsui-OSK]
538'	13.619	ARAMAC [Eastern & Australian]	511'	11.030	GRUZIA [USSR]
538'	12.006	CHARLES TELLIER [Mess Maritimes]	508'	13.803	ATLANTICA [Typaldos]
538'	9.008	ORIENTAL WARRIOR [CY Tung]	508'	9.237	ACROPOLIS [Typaldos]
538'	8.999	ORIENTAL LADY [CY Tung]	508'	9.237	ATHINAI [Typaldos]
538'	8.974	ORIENTAL INVENTOR [CY Tung]	508'	9.971	MONTE UMBE [Aznar]
538'	8.959	ORIENTAL HERO [CY Tung]	507'	10.304	KAMPALA [Br India]
538'	8.955	ORIENTAL RULER [CY Tung]	507'	10.294	KARANJA [Br India]
538'	8.929	ORIENTAL MUSICIAN [CY Tung]	505'	10.946	CHARLESVILLE [Belgian Line]
537'	14.083	AUREOL [Elder Dempster]	505'	10.877	ALBERTVILLE [Belgian Line]
537'	13.204	IRPINIA [Siosa]	505'	10.877	ELISABETHVILLE [Belgian Line]
537'	12.359	LOUIS LUMIERE [Mess Maritimes]	505'	10.877	LEOPOLDVILLE [Belgian Line]
537'	12.007	LAENNEC [Mess Maritimes]	505'	10.854	AUSTRALASIA [Malaysia Line]
532'	13.520	CAMBODGE [Mess Maritimes]	505'	9.828	POBEDA [USSR]
532'	13.520	LAOS [Mess Maritimes]	504'	11.366	DINTELDYK [Holl-Amer]
532'	13.520	VIET-NAM [Mess Maritimes]	503'	15.024	MAASDAM [Holl-Amer]
531'	13.196	PATRIA [Colonial]	503'	15.015	RYNDAM [Holl-Amer]
531'	13.186	IMPERIO [Colonial]	503'	10.723	URUGUAY STAR [Blue Star]
531'	12.457	GENERAL MANGIN [Cie Paquetbots]	503'	10.722	PARAGUAY STAR [Blue Star]
530'	12.653	LIBERTAD [ELMA Lines]	503'	10.716	ARGENTINA MARU [Blue Star]
530'	12.627	URUGUAY [ELMA Lines]	503'	10.716	BRASIL STAR [Blue Star]
528'	13.226	DONIZETTI [Italian]	502'	12.464	FAIRSKY [Sitmar]
528'	13.226	VERDI [Italian]	502'	10.726	OCEANIEN [Mess Maritimes]
528'	13.225	ROSSINI [Italian]	501'	9.853	ANGRA DON HEROSIMO [Emp. Insul.]
528'	10.574	JAGERSFONTEIN [Holl-Africa]	501'	9.824	FUNCHAL [Empresa Insulana]
			501'	9.855	AMELIA DE MELLO [Portugese]

S/S "FRANCE"

PONT DU SOLEIL	① SUN DECK	PONT ATLANTIQUE	⑦ ATLANTIC DECK	FUMOIR	Ⓕ SMOKING ROOM
PONT DES EMBARCATIONS	② BOAT DECK	PONT BORDEAUX	⑧ BORDEAUX DECK	SALON	Ⓢ LOUNGE
PONT VERANDA	③ VERANDAH DECK	PONT DEAUVILLE	⑨ DEAUVILLE DECK	SALLE A MANGER	Ⓜ DINING ROOM
PONT PROMENADE	④ PROMENADE DECK			PISCINE	Ⓟ SWIMMING POOL
PONT SUPERIEUR	⑤ UPPER DECK			THEATRE	Ⓣ THEATRE
PONT PRINCIPAL	⑥ MAIN DECK				

51

AZNAR - AFRICA LINE
HOLLAND - AFRICA LINE
CIE. HAVRAISE PENINSULAIRE

Combination passenger-cargo liners were particularly well-suited to the African trades, for voyages with specialized needs and of long duration with extensive ports of call. First class accommodations were often of high standard, a consideration to those passengers who would have lengthy stays onboard.

Spain's Aznar Line, the Naviera Aznar, offered a popular and profitable service to the Canary Islands (Las Palmas and Teneriffe) from Liverpool and London, often on a seasonal schedule from November through May. Bananas and fruits were important return cargo. Alternately, Company ships went to Latin America or the Caribbean with immigrants and workers.

The Holland-Africa Line used several fine motorliners --- namely the RANDFONTEIN, JAGERSFONTEIN, ORANJE-FONTEIN and BLOEMFONTEIN --- on the South and East African service. Their rather lengthy voyages, which were especially popular with first class holiday passenger traffic, sailed outwards from Hamburg, Antwerp, Amsterdam and Southampton to Capetown, Port Elizabeth, East London, Durban and Lourenco Marques, before returning home to Northern Europe. Like many others, Holland-Africa abandoned such passenger service in the late Sixties, in the face of declining passenger requirements and a change in cargo shipping.

The Nouvelle Compagnie Havraise Peninsulaire de Navigation, headquartered in Paris, used a trio of 27-passenger combo ships on the very extended run out to Madagascar via the Suez. After leaving the Continental ports of Hamburg, Antwerp, Dunkirk, Le Havre, Rouen and Marseilles, the three sisters --- the ILE DE LA REUNION, ILE MAURICE and NOSSI-BE --- sailed onto Algiers and then a transit of the Suez Canel before proceeding to such exotically-named ports as Djibouti, Majunga, Diego-Suarez and Mananjary. This trade continues at present, but with specialty container ships.

ILE MAURICE   Built 1951
Built by: Odense Shipyard,
          Odense, Denmark
8,826 gross tons
476 feet long   60 feet wide
B & W - diesel geared to single screw
Service speed 16 knots
27 first class passengers only

MONTE UDALA   Built 1948
Built by: Compania Euskalduna,
          Bilbao, Spain
10,170 gross tons
487 feet long   62 feet wide
Sulzer diesel geared to single screw
Service speed 16 knots
392 passengers
        62 first class;   40 second class
        290 third class

[LEFT] Aznar Line's MONTE UDALA was built as a freighter but modified to carry passengers, especially immigrants in third class quarters. Like other Aznar passenger vessels, she sailed to South America as well as on the more local trade between Britain and the Canaries. In the latter, she drew profits not only from passenger revenues but from the fresh fruit business as well. [RIGHT] The BLOEMFONTEIN— with its richly sounding Dutch name— was one of several combination liners that sailed the Holland-Africa Line's service between Amsterdam, Southampton and ports in South and East Africa. [BELOW] The French ILE MAURICE was one of a trio owned by the Compagnie Navraise Peninsulaire that sailed between Northern Europe and Madagascar via the Suez. In addition to high standard first class accomodations, the cargo facilities included special wine tanks.

Opposite: Alex Duncan; This page: J. K.Byass; Roger Sherlock.

BLOEMFONTEIN   Built 1934
Built by: Netherlands Shipbuilding Co.,
          Amsterdam, Holland
11,473 gross tons
487 feet long   63 feet wide
Stork diesels geared to twin screw
Service speed 14½ knots
143 passengers
        79 first class;   64 second class

COMPANHIA COLONIAL

The Companhia Colonial of Lisbon, one of Portugal's two most prominent passenger ship operators, was heavily involved in the colonial trade to Angola and Mozambique. Passenger ships such as the INFANTE DOM HENRIQUE, PATRIA, IMPERIO and UIGE sailed from Lisbon out to Sao Tome, Luanda, Lobito and Mossamedes, then rounded the Cape to Lourenco Marques, Beira and Mozambique.

Two other, rather notable Colonial liners --- the handsome SANTA MARIA and VERA CRUZ --- worked on different routes. The SANTA MARIA sailed the mid-Atlantic, from Lisbon to La Guaira, Curacao, San Juan or Havana and then to Port Everglades, Florida. The VERA CRUZ sailed mostly to Brazil --- to Recife, Salvador, Rio and Santos.

Companhia Colonial --- by then merged into a consortium of Portugese ship operators --- closed out all of its passenger sailings by 1976.

When the VERA CRUZ and her sistership, the SANTA MARIA, were delivered in 1952-53, they were by far the largest Portugese-flag liners ever built. With rather high superstructures, both ships made extensive early use of aluminum. The SANTA MARIA made worldwide headline news when she was hijacked by Portugese political terrorists in January 1961. While the SANTA MARIA spent most of her life sailing to the Caribbean and Florida, the VERA CRUZ sailed to Brazil mostly and then spent her final years as a troopship, supporting the troubled Portugese— African colonies.

Companhia Colonial.

VERA CRUZ   Built 1952
Built by: John Cockerill S. A.,
            Hoboken, Belgium
21,765 gross tons
610 feet long   76 feet wide
Steam turbines geared to twin screw
Service speed 20 knots
1098 passengers
         148 first class;   250 cabin class
         700 third class

[ABOVE] The UIGE was built at the same yards as the earlier VERA CRUZ and SANTA MARIA, but was intended mostly for the immigrant trade. However, she was given a small but comfortable first class section, with a mere 78 berths. [BELOW] The sisterships IMPERIO and PATRIA — the first Portugese liners to be built after the Second War — reflected the diversity of the African trades. The intimate first class quarters had to be quite deluxe and ornate whereas, in the extreme, there were separate third class section for immigrants, workers and troops. In addition, each ship was fitted with five sizeable cargo holds.

Michael Cassar; Alex Duncan.

IMPERIO   Built 1948
Built by: John Brown & Company Ltd.,
                 Clydebank, Scotland
13,186 gross tons
532 feet long   68 feet wide
Steam turbines geared to twin screw
Service speed 17 knots
590 passengers
            114 first class;   156 tourist class
            120 third class;   200 fourth class

UIGE   Built 1955
Built by: John Cockerill S. A.,
                 Hoboken, Belgium
10,001 gross tons
477 feet long   63 feet wide
B & W-type diesels geared to single screw
Service speed 16 knots
571 passengers
            78 first class;   493 third class

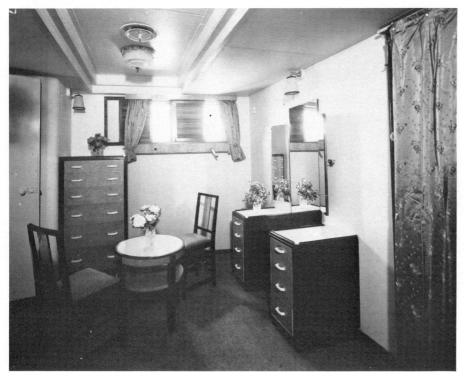

First class quarters aboard the Belgian-built UIGE of the Companhia Colonial included the Main Lounge [ABOVE], the sitting area of a suite [LEFT] and the Verandah [UPPER RIGHT] More typical of the ship's accommodations are the Third Class cabins [BELOW].

Compania Colonial.

EMPRESA INSULANA
COMPANHIA NACIONAL

The Empresa Insulana de Navegacao, also of Lisbon, traded on the more localized runs to Madeira and the Azores. Some aged passenger ships were replaced in 1961 by the new FUNCHAL. Later, as this service dwindled, this latter ship was converted to a cruise liner --- dividing her time between Scandinavia in the summers and South America in winter.

The Companhia Nacional --- the second of Portugal's major liner operators --- restricted most of its services to colonial Africa, to Angola and Mozambique. The flagship PRINCIPE PERFEITO was joined by two large combo liners, the ANGOLA and MOCAMBIQUE, and the somewhat smaller NIASSA. Two further Nacional passenger ships, the INDIA and TIMUR, were the only exceptions. They traded on a more extensive service, from London, Continental ports and Lisbon out to India and the Far East.

Like so many other similar firms, Nacional passenger operations ceased in the mid-Seventies, a result of changing politics and trade requirements.

At this time [1983], regular passenger service to Africa has all but vanished completely. One remaining link is the services of the St. Helena Shipping Company, sailing out of Avonmouth in England to St. Helena and the South African Cape, using the chartered, Singapore-registered CENTAUR, carrying 190 passengers and formerly of the Blue Funnel Line.

[ABOVE] The FUNCHAL was the flagship and largest vessel in the Empresa Insulana service to Madeira and the Azores out of Lisbon. [UPPER RIGHT] The PRINCIPE PERFEITO was the largest and last passenger liner in the Companhia Nacional fleet. In addition to her attractive passenger accommodations, she was fitted with quarters for 200 additional troops should the need arise in the Portugese African colonies. [RIGHT] The NIASSA — also a part of the Companhia Nacional fleet to Portugese Africa — was another typical passenger-cargo combination type. Her tourist class quarters were intended specifically for immigrants while her cargo spaces included special palm oil tanks.

This page: Roger Sherlock. Opposite: Michael D.J. Lennon; Roger Sherlock.

FUNCHAL   Built 1961
Built by: Elsinore Shipbuilding & Engineering
                Company, Elsinore, Denmark
9824 gross tons
501 feet long   63 feet wide
Steam turbines geared to twin screw
Service speed 20 knots
400 passengers
            80 first class;   156 second class
            164 tourist class

PRINCIPE PERFEITO   Built 1961
Built by: Swan, Hunter & Wigham Richardson
                Limited, Newcastle, England
19,393 gross tons
625 feet long   79 feet wide
Steam turbines geared to twin screw
Service speed 20 knots
1000 passengers
            200 first class;   800 tourist class

NIASSA   Built 1955
Built by: Cockerill - Ougree Shipyards,
                Hoboken, Belgium
10,742 gross tons
497 feet long   64 feet wide
Doxford diesels geared to single screw
Service speed 16 knots
306 passengers
            22 first class;   284 tourist class

VENUS   Built 1931
Built by: Elsinore Shipbuilding & Engineering
                Company, Elsinore, Denmark
6,269 gross tons
420 feet long   54 feet wide
B & W-type diesels geared to twin screw
Service speed 19 knots
411 summertime passengers
            133 first class;   277 tourist class
            251 wintertime passengers - first class
            only

[RIGHT] The handsome little NORDST-JERNEN was one of the thirteen passenger-mail ships on the Norwegian coastal trade. [LEFT] The smart-looking motorliner VENUS was an extremely popular and profitable ship. In summer, she sailed the North Sea express route between Newcastle and Bergen. Then, in winter, with her hull repainted white, she traded between Southampton and Madeira with holiday passengers. [BELOW] For their service between Newcastle and Oslo, the Fred Olsen line built the advanced-looking BLENHEIM and BRAEMAR of 1951-53. The specially designed funnel was made of aluminum and was worked into the superstrcture.

This page: Roger Sherlock; Fred Olsen Line.
Opposite: World Ship Collection.

BLENHEIM   Built 1951
Built by: Thornycroft Shipyard,
                Southampton, England
                Completed by Akers Shipyard,
                Oslo, Norway
4,766 gross tons
374 feet long   53 feet wide
B & W-type diesel geared to single screw
Service speed 16½ knots
290 passengers
            100 first class;   130 second class
            60 economy class

CHAPTER FOUR:

LOCAL NORTH SEA AND MEDITERRANEAN SERVICES

BERGEN LINE
FRED OLSEN LINE

Norway's Bergen Line maintained regular North Sea passenger service --- using the small liners LEDA and VENUS for a good number of years --- between Newcastle and Bergen, short-sea voyages taking approximately 19 hours in each direction. In addition, the Company participated in the famed Norwegian costal service --- the "Hurtigruta" --- which sailed out of Bergen to dozens of ports and which went beyond the North Cape to Kirkenes and, on occasion, further to Spitzbergen. Thirteen little passenger vessels maintained this service, one which later became even more popular with round-trip tourists rather than local passengers for whom it was originally intended. Beginning in 1982, the smaller, older ships were gradually replaced by new roll-on, roll-off ferry types.

The Fred Olsen Line --- another Norwegian and with a sizeable cargo operation as well --- also sailed the North Sea, trading between Newcastle and Oslo, via Kristiansand. Their twin mini-liners --- the BLENHEIM and BRAEMAR --- were especially futuristic in design for their time [1951-53], particularly with their disguised smokestack arrangment.

NORDSTJERNEN   Built 1955
Built in Norway
2,193 gross tons
297 feet long   45 feet wide
Diesel geared to single screw
Service speed 16 knots
192 passengers in first and second class

DFDS

Denmark's DFDS --- the United Steamship Company Limited --- traded locally between home waters and Norway, and across the North Sea to England. During the peak summer tourist months, daily voyages were run between Copenhagen and Oslo. On the longer route, between Esbjerg and Harwich, sailings were made as often as six times per week. Each ship was fitted with cargo hold space for automobiles. However, at present, all of those earlier DFDS motorliners have been replaced by much larger car ferries --- often taking over 1,000 passengers each in both cabin accommodation and in airline-type reclining seats. Large garages for several hundred autos are also included.

The KRONPRINSESSE INGRID of DFDS prepares to sail from Copenhagen for a Northern Cities cruise on May 8th 1965. Normally, this ship ran the North Sea shuttle between Esbjerg, Denmark and Harwich in England.

DFDS Seaways.

KRONPRINSESSE INGRID Built 1949
Built by: Elsinore Shipbuilding & Engineering
          Company, Elsinore, Denmark
3,985 gross tons
375 feet long   50 feet wide
B & W-type diesels geared to twin screw
Service speed 20½ knots
334 passengers
          148 first class;   146 second class
          40 third class

ADRIATICA LINE

Italy's state-owned Adriatica Line ran nine very high-standard passenger ships in local Eastern Mediterranean waters. On all but three vessels, passengers were divided into three classes and then each ship also had a good-sized cargo capacity as well. The two largest ships, the AUSONIA and ESPERIA, worked the express run from either Genoa and Naples or Trieste and Venice to Beirut and Alexandria. The sisters ENOTRIA and MESSAPIA alternated, sailing from Genoa and Naples to Piraeus, Cyprus, Haifa and then return to Piraeus, Venice and Trieste, then outbound again but from the Adriatic. The sisters SAN GIORGIO and SAN MARCO traded to Turkish ports --- to Istanbul and Izmir via Piraeus. Finally, an all-first class trio --- the BERNINA, BRENNERO and STELVIO --- balanced a more extensive routing: from Italian ports to Alexandria, Port Said, Beirut, Latakia, Famagusta, Rhodes, Mersin, Izmir and Piraeus.

The AUSONIA of 1957 was the Adriatica Line flagship and largest liner. She sailed on the express run to Alexandria.

Michael D. J. Lennon.

AUSONIA   Built 1957
Built by: Cantieri Riuniti dell 'Adriatico
                          Monfalcone, Italy
11,879 gross tons
522 feet long   70 feet wide
Steam turbines geared to twin screw
Service speed 20 knots
529 passengers
           181 first class;   118 second class
           230 tourist class

FRENCH LINE
TURKISH MARITIME LINE
ZIM LINE

The French Line maintained a seperate fleet of passenger ships, well apart from its Atlantic liners, that sailed the local waters of the western Mediterranean. One group of ships traded out of Marseilles and Nice to Corsica --- to the ports of Ajacco, Bastia, Ile Rousse and Calvi. The alternate set of ships went to colonial Algeria --- to Oran, Algiers, Philippeville and Bone.

The Turks --- namely the Turkish Maritime Lines --- maintained a fleet of passenger-cargo liners on several Mediterranean routes. Services were run from Istanbul and Izmir as far west as Marseilles, Genoa and Naples; another to Trieste and Venice; and still another to Alexandria and Tripoli.

Israel's state shipping company, the Zim Lines, ran several passenger ships between Marseilles and Haifa. For some years, the immigrant run with new settlers to Israel was booming. In addition, there was also a seasonal tourist trade. However, in later years, the high expense of operating Israeli passenger ships far exceeded the passenger revenues. The Zim Lines sensibly withdrew to cargo shipping only.

MOLEDET   Built 1961
Built by: Ateliers et Chantiers de Bretagne,
           Nantes, France
7,811 gross tons
415 feet long   65 feet wide
S.E.M.T.-Pielstick diesels geared to single screw
Service speed 16 knots
590 tourist class passengers

[LEFT] **In addition to service on the Zim Lines'
run between southern France, Italy, Greece
and Israel, the MOLEDET also made occasional cruises.** [RIGHT] **The Turkish IZMIR
represented the varied needs of a Mediterranean passenger cargo vessel trading between
Italian and Greek ports and Istanbul. The
passenger accommodations were divided between four classes—from a very comfortable
first class that included two suites, to deck
quarters for pilgrims and workers. In addition, she carried cargo in four good-sized
holds and had space for 34 automobiles.**
[BELOW] **The SAMPIERO CORSO was one of
the French Line passenger ships which handled
the trade out of Marseilles to Corsica. In later
years, this route became the domain of car
ferries with drive-on, drive-off capabilities.**

*Opposite: Zim Lines. This page: Michael D.J.
Lennon; French Line.*

SAMPIERO CORSO   Built 1936
Built by: Chantiers & Ateliers de Provence
           Port de Bouc, France
4041 gross tons
345 feet long   48 feet wide
Steam turbines geared to twin screw
Service speed 15½ knots
824 passengers
           113 first class;   115 third class
           596 fourth class

IZMIR   Built 1955
Built by: A.G. Weser Shipyards,
           Bremerhaven, West Germany
6,049 gross tons
402 feet long   54 feet wide
M.A.N. type diesel geared to single screw
Service speed 14 knots
796 passengers
           72 first class;   72 second class;
           332 tourist class;   320 deck passengers

TIRRENIA LINE
EFTHYMIADIS LINE
HELLENIC MEDITERRANEAN LINES

Another of Italy's state-owned passenger firms, the Tirrenia Line, was involved with Central Mediterranean services --- to Tunisia, Sicily and also Sardinia. The Greeks had, of course, built up a large fleet of ships for both local Aegean services as well as more far-flung Mediterranean operations. The Efthymiadis Lines --- which developed a series of ferry services across the Adriatic from Italy and out of Piraeus to the Greek islands, particularly to Crete --- were rather noteworthy for converting several former Norwegian oil tankers for passenger and auto work. The tanks and most of the innards were removed and replaced by large garages, cabins, dormitories and lounges.

Other Greek-flag firms, such as the Hellenic Mediterranean Lines, offered an extended link between Marseilles, Genoa, Naples, Piraeus, Beirut, Alexandria and Port Said. During the Fifties and Sixties, in a time before the more specialized car ferry, aged passenger ships --- such as the IONIA of 1913 --- were perfectly suited for such services. However, at present, with a vast change in passenger and tourist requirements, such new ferries --- with large garages, stern-loading doors, swimming pools, discos, closed circuit television and mini-supermarkets --- are far more common to Mediterranean waters.

[ABOVE] **Tirrenia Line's LAZIO, one of seven sisters which worked the Company's varied Central Mediterranean passenger services.** [UPPER RIGHT] **The Greek-flag Efthymiadis Lines were notable in taking several Norwegian tankers and converting them to passenger and car carriers for the Aegean inter-island trades. The SOPHIA was the former SOYA BIRGITTA and was converted in 1966.** [RIGHT] **Built originally in 1913 as the Furness Lines' DIGBY, the IONA finished her long career as the flagship of the Hellenic Mediterranean Lines. She worked the firm's express service between the south of France, Italy, Greece, Lebanon and Egypt—assisted by an assortment of other older vessels. Again, the demands of this trade were varied—from first class to very inexpensive dormitory accomodations to deck spaces without berths.**

This page: Roger Sherlock. Opposite: Michael Casser; World Ship Society Collection.

LAZIO   Built 1955
Built by: Cantieri Navali Riuniti Shipyard
           Palermo, Italy
5,230 gross tons
383 feet long   52 feet wide
Fiat diesels geared to twin screw
Service speed 16¾ knots
560 passengers in three classes

SOPHIA   Built 1953
Built in Norway
9,005 gross tons
496 feet long   62 feet wide
Diesels geared to single screw
Service speed 15 knots
670 passengers; 200 autos

IONIA   Built 1913
Built by: Irving Shipbuilding & Drydock Co.,
           Hartlepool, England
5,375 gross tons
367 feet long   50 feet wide
Steam triple expansion engines geared to
single screw
Service speed 14 knots
520 passengers
           66 first class;   219 tourist class
           84 dormitory;   151 deck passengers

TYPALDOS LINES

Another large Greek operator was the Typaldos Lines. While its larger ships --- the ACROPOLIS and ATHINAI, the former SANTA PAULA and SANTA ROSA of 1932 and from the American Grace Line --- were often detoured to cruising, other services were run from Venice to Greece and Israel, between Piraeus and Heraklion on Crete, out to Istanbul and locally from Piraeus to the Aegean isles. At its peak, the Company had over ten passenger ships, all of which had seen earlier lives from previous owners. However, in December 1966, the Typaldos ferry HERAKLION sank with the loss of 241 lives. Negligence was found during the inquiry that followed, the owners were jailed and the Typaldos fleet was seized (and later partially disbanded) by the Greek Government.

The Typaldos liner ATHINAI was used for extensive cruising—to Scandinavia in the summers and at other times to West Africa, the Aegean and Black Seas.

Alex Duncan.

ATHINAI   Built 1932
Built by: Newport News Shipbuilding &
          Drydock Co.,
          Newport News, Virginia, USA
9,237 gross tons
508 feet long   72 feet wide
Steam turbines geared to twin screw
Service speed 17½ knots
Approximately 500 passengers

CHAPTER FIVE:
THE SOVIET FLEET

BLACK SEA STATE STEAMSHIP COMPANY
SOVIET MINISTRY OF SHIPPING

The Soviets began their large passenger ship build-up soon after the Second World War, mostly with seized or salvaged former Nazi-German tonnage. The biggest of these, the onetime transatlantic liner ALBERT BALLIN, was resurected as the SOVETSKY SOJUS. Then, in 1958, the nineteen sisters and near-sisters of the MIKHAIL KALININ class were begun and ranked as the first notable, brand-new Soviet passenger ship project. Although they were quite small by world standards, these ships were so designed not only for passenger service --- in the Baltic, across the North Sea, in the Mediterranean and Black Seas, and in the Far East --- but for a diverse range of other roles including research missions, Polar supply and even trooping if needed. In 1964, East German yards began production of larger, 20,000-ton sisterships --- the IVAN FRANKO, TARAS SCHEVCHENKO, ALEXANDR PUSHKIN, SHOTA RUSTAVELLI and later the MIKHAIL LERMONTOV --- for even greater deep-sea which have included British charters to Australia with immigrants, considerable cruising for the likes of the West Germans and Dutch, even regular summertime Atlantic services to Montreal and New York. Successive generations of Soviet passenger ships --- coming mostly out of Finland or

East Germany --- have given that country the largest passenger fleet in the world by the early Eighties [over 35 ships in 1980]. Although they sometimes sail under a commercial banner, such as the Black Sea State Steamship Company, or under foreign charter, all of these ships are state-owned, by the Soviet Ministry of Shipping in Moscow.

The BALTIKA made a special Atlantic crossing to New York in 1960 with then Soviet Premier Nikita Khruschev onboard.

Roger Sherlock.

BALTIKA   Built 1940
Built by: Netherlands Shipbuilding Company,
                  Amsterdam, Holland
7,494 gross tons
445 feet long   60 feet wide
Steam turbo-electric geared to twin screw
Service speed 16 knots
436 passengers
           76 first class;   360 tourist class

ALEXANDR PUSHKIN   Built 1965
Built by: Mathias-Thesen Werft,
              Wismar, East Germany
19,860 gross tons
577 feet long   77 feet wide
Sulzer diesels geared to twin screw
Service speed 20 knots
666 passengers
              86 first class;   580 tourist class

ABKHAZIA   Built 1939
Built by: Stettiner Oderwerke Shipyard,
              Stettin, Germany
6,807 gross tons
430 feet long   60 feet wide
Steam turbo-electric geared to twin screw
Service speed 15 knots
548 passengers
              66 first class;   188 second class
              294 third class

[ABOVE] **The ABKHAZIA docked at the Passenger Ship Terminal at Batumi.** [LOWER LEFT] **In 1966, the ALEXANDR PUSHKIN reopened Soviet transatlantic service by sailing between Leningrad and Montreal.** [UPPER RIGHT] **The Passenger Terminal at Batumi with two ex-German liners at dock; the POBEDA is in the foreground, the ROSSIA beyond.** [RIGHT] **The ROSSIA docking at New York, during one of her special visits there in the late forties.**

This Page: Herbert G. Frank Jr.; Michael Cassar. Opposite: Vincent Messina collection; Frank O. Braynard collection.

ROSSIA   Built 1938
Built by: Deutsche Werft Shipyard
              Hamburg, Germany
17,870 gross tons
584 feet long   74 feet wide
Diesel electric engines geared to twin screw
Service speed 16 knots

POBEDA   Built 1928
Built by: F. Schichau Shipyard,
               Danzig, Germany
9,828 gross tons
505 feet long   61 feet wide
Sulzer diesel geared to twin screw
Service speed 14½ knots
1004 passengers
          56 first class;   130 second class
          218 third class;   600 deck passengers

TS. Maxim Gorky

BLACK SEA SHIPPING COMPANY

MIKHAIL KALININ   Built 1958
Built by: Mathias-Thesen Werft,
              Wismar, East Germany
4,722 gross tons
401 feet long   18 feet wide
M.A.N. type diesels geared to twin screw
Service speed 18 knots
333 one-class passengers

FEODOR SHALYAPIN   Built 1955
Built by: John Brown & Co Ltd.,
              Clydebank, Scotland
22,637 gross tons
608 feet long   80 feet wide
Steam turbines geared to twin screw
Service speed 19½ knots
Approximately 850 one-class passengers

[ABOVE] The **MIKHAIL KALININ was the first in a class of 19 similar passenger ships, specifically designed for a wide range of services—from regular liner voyages to cruising, trooping, Polar research and replenishment, trade-goodwill missions.**
[BELOW] The **FEODOR SHALYAPIN—the former Cunarder FRANCONIA—has been used for a variety of roles: cruises from Britain and Australia, for workers and technicians, and for the movement of Cuban troops to East Africa and the Middle East. In this scene, she is docked at the Yokohama Ocean Terminal, during a cruise from Sydney, and with the Japanese ferry MARIMO in the background.**

Alex Duncan; M. Yamada.

CHAPTER SIX:

THE INDIAN OCEAN

BRITISH INDIA LINE

The diversity of possible Indian Ocean passenger services was perhaps best exemplified by the British India Steam Navigation Company Limited, itself a reflection of the once extensive British Empire. ''BI'' --- as they most commonly know --- had a fleet of passenger ships based mostly in India, usually at Bombay. The sisterships KARANJA and KAMPALA, and the AMRA and ARONDA sailed out to the Seychelles and then to East Africa. The trio of SANGOLA, SIRDHANA and SANTHIA worked from Calcutta to Malaysia and then northwards to Hong Kong and Japan. The veteran RAJULA of 1926 handled the relay between Madras and Singapore. Finally, the four sisters of the ''D Class'' --- the DARA, DARESSA, DUMRA and DWARKA --- put out of Bombay and Karachi to ports along the Persian Gulf.

By 1982, British India was reduced to two passenger ships: the schoolship UGANDA (formerly on the London-East Africa trade) and the little DWARKA, the last survivor of the former Persian Gulf run. A year later, both were out of service, marking the end of the once vast British India fleet.

British India's SANTHIA sits at anchor at Hong Kong.

P. & O. Group.

SANTHIA   Built 1956
Built by: Barclay Curle & Company,
                  Glasgow, Scotland
8,908 gross tons
479 feet long   63 feet wide
Doxford Diesels geared to twin screw
Service speed 14½ knots
1193 passengers
               25 first class;   70 second class
               68 intermediate;   268 bunk class
               762 deck passengers

ROYAL ROTTERDAM LLOYD NEDERLAND LINE

The Dutch --- namely the Royal Rotterdam Lloyd and the Nederland Line --- maintained a major passenger service to the East Indies, even after the radical political changes and the creation of present-day Indonesia. Several large liners --- notably the WILLEM RUYS, ORANJE and JOHAN VAN OLDENBARNEVELT --- sailed outwards from either Rotterdam or Amsterdam and Southampton to the Mediterranean and then through Suez for Djakarta. However, by the late Fifties, the service was expanded to completely circle the globe, using the Panama Canal route as well. But, the competion was stiff, particularly from Britain's diverse P&O Lines. The WILLEM RUYS and ORANJE were sold off to the Italians and rebuilt to start new lives on the Australian run. The JOHAN VAN OLDENBARNEVELT went to the Greeks, but only to be lost in a grizzly Christmas Cruise fire off Madeira in December 1963. She was then known as the LAKONIA.

[ABOVE] The WILLEM RUYS was the first major liner to have her lifeboats stowed inboard on a low deck, rather than in more obvious davits on the customary, upper Boat Deck. After finishing her Dutch service in 1964, she was sold to the Lauro Line of Italy and was drastically rebuilt as their ACHILLE LAURO.

Herbert G. Frank, Jr. Collection.

WILLEM RUYS   Built 1947
Built by: De Schelde Shipyard,
             Flushing, Holland
23,114 gross tons
631 feet long   82 feet wide
Sulzer diesels geared to twin screw
Service speed 22 knots
1045 passengers
         275 first class;   770 tourist class

ORANJE   Built 1939
Built by: Netherlands Shipbuilding Company,
             Amsterdam, Holland
20,551 gross tons
656 feet long   83 feet wide
Sulzer diesels geared to triple screw
Service speed 21½ knots
949 passengers
         323 first class;   626 tourist class

ALSO SEE ANGELINA LAURO ON PAGE 88

JOHAN VAN OLDENBARNEVELT
                      Built 1930
Built by: Netherlands Shipbuilding Company,
             Amsterdam, Holland
19,787 gross tons
608 feet long   74 feet wide
Sulzer diesels geared to twin screw
Service speed 17 knots
1414 one - class passengers

[ABOVE] **The ORANJE of the Nederland Line
was also sold to the Lauro Line in 1964 and
she too was thoroughly rebuilt.** [BELOW] **The
JOHAN VAN OLDENBARNEVELT—
commonly referred more simply as the
"JVO"— was probably the most popular
and beloved of the Dutch East Indian
liners.**

Roger Sherlock; Skyfotos Limited.

BIBBY LINE

The **WARWICKSHIRE** of Britain's Bibby Line sailed between Liverpool and Rangoon via Suez.

World Ship Society Collection.

WARWICKSHIRE   Built 1948
Built by: Fairfield Shipbuilding & Engineering
                Company, Glasgow Scotland
Steam turbine geared to single screw
Service speed 14½ knots
76 first class passengers

GLEN LINE

The **DENBIGHSHIRE** of the British Glen Line sailed outwards from British and European ports by way of Suez to Malaya, Hong Kong, China and Japan.

Alex Duncan.

DENBIGHSHIRE   Built 1938
Built by: Netherlands Shipbuilding Company,
                Amsterdam, Holland
6,983 gross tons
507 feet long   66 feet wide
B&W type diesels geared to twin screw
Service speed 17 knots
18 first class passengers

BLUE FUNNEL LINE

The **PYRRHUS** was one of four sisters which worked Blue Funnel Line's trade out of Liverpool and Rotterdam via Suez to Singapore, Manila, Hong Kong, Kobe and Yokohama.

J.K. Byass.

PYRRHUS   Built 1949
Built by: Cammell Laird & Co. Ltd.,
                Birkenhead, England
10,093 gross tons
516 feet long   68 feet wide
Steam turbines geared to single screw
Service speed 18½ knots
30 first class passengers

ANCHOR LINE

The CALEDONIA— the last passenger ship to be built for the Anchor Line— sailed from Liverpool out to Gibraltar, Port Said, Aden, Karachi and Bombay.

Michael D.J. Lennon.

CALEDONIA   Built 1948
Built by: Fairfield Shipbuilding & Engineering,
              Company, Glasgow, Scotland
11,225 gross tons
506 feet long   66 feet wide
Doxford diesels geared to twin screw
Service speed 16 knots
304 first class passengers

EAST ASIATIC COMPANY

Owned by Denmark's East Asiatic Company, the SELANDIA and several of her fleetmates were known as the "stackless" ships. The exhausts were worked through pipes in the third mast. The routing was from Copenhagen and other intermediate ports out to Bangkok and Saigon.

Alex Duncan.

SELANDIA   Built 1945
Built by: Nakskov Shipyard
              Nakskov, Denmark
8,454 gross tons
452 feet long   63 feet wide
B & W type diesels geared to single screw
Service speed 15 knots
64 first class passengers

HAMBURG - AMERICAN LINE

The Hamburg-American Line and North German Lloyd combined their efforts with six combination ships for their Europe-Suez-Far East route. Like the FRANK-FURT, each of them offered high standard accomodations.

Roger Sherlock.

FRANKFURT   Built 1954
Built by: Bremer Vulkan Shipyards,
              Bremen, Germany
8,959 gross tons
538 feet long   64 feet wide
M.A.N. type diesel geared to single screw
Service speed 16½ knots
86 first class passengers

ROYAL INTEROCEAN LINES

Holland's Royal Interocean Lines rarely went to home waters, but instead offered some of the most extensive liner routes in the world. Three of the principal ships --- the BOISSE-VAIN, RUYS and TEGELBERG --- sailed from Rio, Santos, Montevideo and Buenos Aires, and then across to Capetown and Durban, before proceeding to Singapore, Djakarta, Hong Kong, Kobe and Yokohama --- voyages touching on three diverse continents. Other Company passenger ships sailed northwards from Australian ports to the Philippines, Hong Kong and Japan, and still others, also from Australia, to Malaysia and India.

BOISSEVAIN   Built 1937
Built by: Blohm & Voss Shipbuilders,
                   Hamburg, Germany
14,285 gross tons
559 feet long   72 feet wide
Sulzer diesels geared to triple screw
Service speed 16 knots
386 passengers in three classes

[ABOVE] The BOISSEVAIN— shown at Durban— was one of Royal Interocean's three express ships on the long-haul South America-South Africa-Far East run. The other sisters were the RUYS and TEGELBERG. [LEFT] The small combination style TJINEGARA, also of Royal Interocean, sailed between India and Australia.

Michael Cassar; Alex Duncan.

TJINEGARA   Built 1952
Built by: P. Smit, Jr. Shipyard,
                   Rotterdam, Holland
9,067 gross tons
472 feet long   64 feet wide
B&W - type diesels geared to single screw
Service speed 16 knots
40 first class passengers

PEACETIME TROOPSHIPS

Peacetime troopships --- for the military, their families and dependents --- were commonplace after the Second World War, particularly with the British and Americans. However, changing politics and the general swing toward air-lifting personnel mostly eliminated the tasks for these ships. The British abandoned regular trooping by sea in the mid-Sixties while Americans followed in the early Seventies. A notable and most unexpected reoccurance of trooping by ship took place in the spring and summer of 1982, when several passenger vessels --- including the QUEEN ELIZABETH 2, CANBERRA and UGANDA --- were specially requisitioned by the British Government for duty in the South Atlantic, during the Falklands crisis.

PASTEUR   Built 1939
Built by: Chantiers de l'Atlantique,
               St. Nazaire France
30,447 gross tons
697 feet long   88 feet wide
Steam turbines geared to quadruple screw
Service speed 23 knots
4500 peacetime troops
        ALSO SEE BREMEN ON PAGE 20

[ABOVE] **The PASTEUR was intended for the South American luxury trade but spent her entire career under the Tricolor as a trooper. Between 1945 and 1957, she sailed mostly out to Indo-China.** [LEFT] **The EMPIRE FOWEY was one of numerous post-war troopships operated by Britain's Ministry of Transport. However, the operational management was given over to commercial firms. The EMPIRE FOWEY came under the houseflag of P & O.**

Both photos: Roger Sherlock.

EMPIRE FOWEY   Built 1935
Built by: Blohm & Voss Shipbuilders
               Hamburg, Germany
19,121 gross tons
634 feet long   74 feet wide
Steam turbines geared to twin screw
Service speed 17 knots
1659 passengers
        347 passengers;   1312 troops
ALSO SEE SAFINA-E-HUJJAJ ON PAGE 81

PILGRIM SHIPS

Many older passenger ships found special work in the pilgrim trades, particularly in Eastern and Indian Ocean waters. Most populus was the Moslem trade to Jeddah. [ABOVE] China Navigation Company's KUALA LUMPUR—the former British troopship DILWARA—spent half of her year in pilgrim service and the remainder on South Pacific cruises. [LEFT] The German East Africa liner PRETORIA found new life after the War—first as a British troopship and then pilgrim ship, and then finally as an Indonesian pilgrim ship, the GUNUNG DJATI. She is shown with only one funnel in place while undergoing an extensive refit at Hong Kong in 1973. [UPPER RIGHT] The former French colonial liner GENERAL MANGIN passed to a number of second owners beginning in the late sixties. For a time, she worked the East Asian pilgrim trades as the EASTERN QUEEN for Singapore owners but flying the Panamanian flag. [RIGHT] Another prewar German—the POTSDAM of the Hamburg-American Line—passed into British hands in 1945 and became the EMPIRE FOWEY. In 1960, she went to Pakistani buyers and became the SAFINA-E-HUJJAJ, mostly for the Karachi-Jeddah run.

This page: Roger Sherlock; Hisashi Noma. Opposite: Michael D.J. Lennon; World Ship Society Collection.

GUNUNG DJATI   Built 1936
Built by: Blohm & Voss Shipbuilders,
                Hamburg, Germany
17,516 gross tons
577 feet long   72 feet wide
Steam turbines geared to twin screw
Service speed 18 knots
2106 passengers, one class
                106 first class;   2000 pilgrims

KUALA LUMPUR   Built 1936
Built by: Barclay, Curle & Co. Ltd.,
           Glasgow, Scotland
12,598 gross tons
517 feet long   63 feet wide
Doxford diesels geared to twin screw
Service speed 14½ knots
1912 passengers
        243 first class;   1669 pilgrims

EASTERN QUEEN   Built 1953
Built by: Chantiers de l'Atlantique
           St. Nazaire, France
11,684 gross tons
531 feet long   65 feet wide
B&W-type diesels geared to twin screw
Service speed 16 knots
Over 1000 passengers

SAFINA-E-HUJJAJ   Built 1935
Built by: Blohm & Voss Shipbuilders,
          Hamburg, Germany
19,116 gross tons
634 feet long   74 feet wide
Steam turbines geared to twin screw
Service speed 17 knots
2602 passengers
        166 first class;   295 second class
        2,141 pilgrims
ALSO SEE EMPIRE FOWEY ON PAGE 79

ORIANA   Built 1960
Built by: Vickers-Armstrong Shipbuilders
             Ltd., Barrow-in-Furness, England
41,923 gross tons
804 feet long   97 feet wide
Steam turbines geared to twin screw
Service speed 27½ knots
2134 passengers
              688 first class;   1496 tourist class

[RIGHT] **P&O's CANBERRA is the largest liner ever built for a service other than the North Atlantic. Her twin aft uptakes and superb sense of structural design have made her an ageless ship.** [ABOVE] **The ORIANA ranks as the fastest liner ever to sail to Australia, reducing the passage time from four to three weeks. She was also the last passenger ship to be built for the Orient Line before its merger with P&O.** [BELOW] **The First Class Ballroom Gallery was bright and modern on the ORIANA.**

All photos: P&O Group.

THE PACIFIC

P & O - ORIENT LINES

Following their merger in 1960, the P&O and Orient lines --- restyled for a time as the P&O-Orient Lines --- had the largest liner fleet on earth, sixteen passenger ships in all: ORSOVA, ORONSAY, ORCADES, ORION, ORONTES, IBERIA, ARCADIA, HIMALAYA, CHUSAN, CANTON, STRATHEDEN, STRATHMORE, STRATHNAVER, STRATHAIRD, CORFU and CARTHAGE. In quick time, this group was to be joined by the largest P&O-Orient liners yet, the ORIANA and CANBERRA.

This combined effort assuredly created the greatest passenger ship schedule as well. England to Australia (and often on to New Zealand) was still the basic trade, but variations and extensions in sailings placed P&O liners in South Africa, the Far East, the Caribbean and Panama, the West Coast of North America, Florida and even along the East Coast of South America. Any other areas not included in the regular liner operation were most likely a part of the alternate, ever-expanding cruise division of P&O.

However, beginning in 1972, with the advanced retirement of the eighteen-year-old IBERIA, P&O long-distance services became noticeably hard-hit by aircraft competition. In quick succession, most of their liners were withdrawn, often sold to the scrappers of Taiwan. At present, with such ships as the CANBERRA and ORIANA, the Company is primarily a one-class cruise operator, sailing either from Southampton or Sidney.

CANBERRA   Built 1961
Built by: Harland & Wolff Limited,
         Belfast, Northern Ireland
45,733 gross tons
818 feet long   87 feet wide
Steam turbo-electric geared to twin screw
Service speed 27½ knots
2272 passengers
       556 first class;   1716 tourist class

[ABOVE] **Three P&O-Orient liners along the Western Docks at Southampton: ORONSAY (left), CANBERRA (middle) and ORCADES (right).** [LEFT] **Even at over 24,000 tons, the CHUSAN was actually one of the smaller liners of the P&O fleet.** [RIGHT] **A splendidly dramatic aerial photograph of P&O's ARCADIA, outbound from London for the Suez, India, Ceylon and Australia.**

This page: H.J. Wood; J.F. Rodriguez.
Opposite: P&O Group.

CHUSAN   Built 1950
Built by: Vickers - Armstrong Shipbuilders
                  Ltd., Barrow - in Furness, England
24,215 gross tons
672 feet long   85 feet wide
Steam turbines geared to twin screw
Service speed 22 knots
1026 passengers
            475 first class;   551 tourist class

ARCADIA   Built 1954
Built by: John Brown & Co. Ltd.,
                  Clydebank, Scotland
29,734 gross tons
721 feet long   91 feet wide
Steam turbines geared to twin screw
Service speed 22 knots
1382 passengers
            647 first class;   735 tourist class

P. & O. 'STRATHEDEN' 1st CLASS SPORTS DECK

P. & O. 'STRATHEDEN' 1st CLASS VERANDAH CAFE

STRATHEDEN   Built 1937
Built by: Vickers-Armstrong Shipbuilders
           Ltd., Barrow-in-Furness, England
23,732 gross tons
664 feet long   84 feet wide
Steam turbines geared to twin screw
Service speed 20 knots
980 passengers
       527 first class;   453 tourist class

Pre-war P&O: The Sports Deck [LEFT] **and
Verandah Cafe** [BELOW LEFT] **onboard the
STRATHEDEN, one of the four surviving
"Straths"—the others being STRATH-
MORE, STRATHNAVER and STRATHAIRD.
More reflections of an older P&O style: The
Bureau on the CARTHAGE** [RIGHT] **and a
First Class Single Stateroom on the
STRATHEDEN** [BELOW]. **Both ships survived
until the early Sixties.**

All photos; James Sesta Collection.

P. & O. 'CARTHAGE' THE BUREAU

'STRATHEDEN' 1st. CLASS SINGLE BERTH CABIN

LAURO LINE
SHAW SAVILL LINE

The Australian immigrant trade continued to boom well into the Sixties. Under Government fare-assisted passages, new settlers could sail out to Fremantle, Melbourne or Sydney for as little as $50 per person. In return, selected companies were given subsidized contracts. This meant guaranteed employment for several large liners.

Italy's Lauro Line added two former Dutch liners --- the vastly rebuilt ACHILLE LAURO and ANGELINA LAURO --- for sailings from Bremerhaven, Rotterdam, Southampton, Genoa and Naples to Australia (and New Zealand) via the Suez. Homewards, these ships somtimes used the Panama route or went via the Straits of Magellan and put in at Buenos Aires and Rio.

The Shaw Savill Line of London --- long interested in the Australia-New Zealand trades --- sailed several fine passenger ships, including the SOUTHERN CROSS and NORTHERN STAR, both of which used the engines-and therefore smokestack-aft design. They were both all-tourist class ships, well suited with a large number of family cabins with four-, six- and eight-berths. They worked as a team, each making four round-the-world voyages per year --- sailing outwards from Southampton via Panama or South Africa, then to Australia and New Zealand, and finally homeward on the alternate route.

Like most other firms on the Australian run, serious decline set-in in the early Seventies. Lauro, for example, turned completely to cruising in 1973 whereas Shaw Savill abandoned passenger services completely two years later.

NORTHERN STAR   Built 1962
Built by: Vickers - Armstrong Shipbuilders
           Ltd., Newcastle, England
24,731 gross tons
650 feet long   83 feet wide
Steam turbines geared to twin screw
Service speed 20 knots
1437 tourist class passengers

ANGELINA LAURO   Built 1939
Built by: Netherlands Shipbuilding Co.,
           Amsterdam, Holland
24,377 gross tons
674 feet long   83 feet wide
Sulzer diesels geared to triple screw
Service speed 21 knots
1616 passengers
          189 first class;   1427 tourist class

ALSO SEE ORANJE ON PAGE 75

[LEFT] **The engines-aft NORTHERN STAR was the last new passenger ship to be built for the Shaw Savill Line. The former Dutch liners WILLEM RUYS** [ABOVE] **and ORANJE** [BELOW] **were superbly transformed into the sleek Lauro Line running-mates ACHILLE LAURO and ANGELINA LAURO respectively. Both conversions took place in the mid-sixties.**

Opposite: Michael D.J. Lennon. This page both photos: Roger Sherlock.

ACHILLE LAURO   Built 1947
Built by: De Schelde Shipyard,
                Flushing, Holland
23,629 gross tons
631 feet long   82 feet wide
Sulzer diesels geared to twin screw
Service speed 22 knots
1307 passengers
          152 first class   1155 tourist class
ALSO SEE WILLEM RUYS ON PAGE 74.

CHANDRIS LINE

The Greek Chandris Brothers started Australian liner service in 1959, under the initial banner of the Europe-Australia Line. Quick success and a roster of passenger ships followed --- the PATRIS, BRITTANY, ELLINIS, AUSTRALIS, QUEEN FREDERICA and BRITANIS. Sailing from Southampton mostly (along with Bremerhaven, Rotterdam, Naples and Piraeus), these ships often went completly full to Australia. To Company accountants, a capacity-filled outbound trip even covered the costs for an otherwise half-full homeward run. While all of the Chandris liners were second-hand, mostly former American, they were very popular ships with casual atmospheres that appealed to many immigrants. The Line was the final passenger ship firm to hold the Australian Government's fare-assisted immigrant contract. The AUSTRALIS made the last run, from Southampton to Sydney, in November 1977.

BRITTANY   Built 1952
Built by: Chantiers de l'Atlantique,
               St. Nazaire, France
16,335 gross tons
581 feet long   73 feet wide
Steam turbines geared to twin screw
Service speed 18 knots
1200 passengers
            150 first class;   1050 tourist class

PATRIS   Built 1950
Built by: Harland Wolff Ltd.,
               Belfast, Northern Ireland
16,259 gross tons
595 feet long   76 feet wide
B & W type diesels geared to twin screw
Service speed 18½ knots
1036 passengers
            36 first class;   1000 tourist class

ELLINIS   Built 1931
Built by: Bethlehem Steel Corporation,
            Quincy, Massachusetts, USA
24,351 gross tons
642 feet long   79 feet wide
Steam turbines geared to twin screw
Service speed 20 knots
1642 tourist class passengers

[LEFT] The ELLINIS—long popular on the Australian run—was the former Matson liner LURLINE, well known on the California-Hawaii circuit. [LOWER LEFT] The French BRETAGNE was first chartered to Chandris and then bought outright, becoming the BRITTANY. Unfortunately, she survived for only two further years. In March 1963, she was destroyed by a drydock fire in Greece. [ABOVE] The AUSTRALIS—the former AMERICA of the United States Lines and onetime flagship of the entire American Merchant Marine—joined Chandris in 1965. [BELOW] The PATRIS was the first of the Chandris Australian liners, added in 1959, after having been the BLOEMFONTEIN CASTLE for Union-Castle.

Opposite: Both photos Roger Sherlock. This page: Michael Cassar; Roger Sherlock.

AUSTRALIS   Built 1940
Built by: Newport News Shipbuilding &
            Drydock Co.,
            Newport News, Virginia, USA
34,449 gross tons
723 feet long   93 feet wide
Steam turbines geared to twin screw
Service speed 22 knots
2258 tourist class passengers

ALSO SEE AMERICA ON PAGE 8

NEW ZEALAND SHIPPING COMPANY

Plying the long-haul trade for the New Zealand Shipping Company between London and Wellington via the Caribbean and Panama was the combination REMUERA, the former Cunarder PARTHIA. Other noted ships on this service included the RANGITANE, RANGITOTO and RUAHINE.

P & O Group

REMUERA   Built 1948
Built by: Harland & Wolff Limited,
          Belfast, Northern Ireland
13,619 gross tons
531 feet long   70 feet wide
Steam turbines geared to twin screw
Service speed 18 knots
350 one-class passengers

MITSUI - O.S.K. LINES

Once the Allied restrictions on post-war ship-building were lifted, the Japanese --- namely the Mitsui-O.S.K. Lines --- opted to develop the passenger-immigrant service to South America, rather than their traditional pre-war service to North America. The resettlement of tens of thousands of Japanese migrants and workers continued until the late Sixties. Among Japan's three post-war passenger ships, two survive as museum and recreation vessels --- the HIKAWA MARU of 1930 at Yokohama and the BRAZIL MARU from 1954 at Toba.

[TOP] The ARGENTINA MARU—seen sailing from Kobe—was the largest post-war liner built for the extensive Japan-U.S.A.-South American run. [LEFT] The ARGENTINA MARU finished her career as the budget cruiseship NIPPON MARU. [RIGHT] Although built as a freighter, the SANTOS MARU was refitted for passenger service.

Two photos: Hisashi Noma. One photo: Hisashi Noma Collection.

ARGENTINA MARU   Built 1958
Built by: Mitsubishi Shipyards,
         Kobe, Japan
10,864 gross tons
513 feet long   67 feet wide
Steam turbines geared to single screw
Service speed 16½ knots
1055 passengers
        23 cabin class   72 tourist class
        960 third class

SANTOS MARU   Built 1952
Built by: Mitsubishi Shipyards,
         Kobe, Japan
8,516 gross tons
475 feet long   105 feet wide
Sulzer diesel geared to single screw
Service speed 14½ knots
614 passengers
        12 cabin class;   44 third class
        558 steerage

SITMAR LINE
LLOYD TRIESTINO
COGEDAR LINE

Other Italian liner companies which participated in the Australian immigrant trade included the Sitmar, Lloyd Triestino and Cogedar lines.

The Sitmar ships --- namely the CASTEL FELICE, FAIRSEA, FAIRSKY and FAIRSTAR --- sailed outwards from Southampton, England (omitting Italian ports entirely) for the Suez Canal and then onwards to Fremantle, Adelaide, Melbourne and Sydney. Occasional runs were extended to include Auckland and Wellington. The ships then returned to England either by way of Singapore and Suez or, creating a full world voyage, via Tahiti, Panama and the Caribbean. Sitmar phased-out its Australian liner services in the early Seventies and turned completely to cruising.

The Lloyd Triestino liners --- the GALILEO GALILEI and GUGLIELMO MARCONI, being the largest --- sailed from both Genoa and Naples, also via the Suez, to Australia, A return call at Bombay was also included. Other Company passenger ships traded to the Far East, as far as Hong Kong, and still two others to South and East Africa, again using Suez. Lloyd Triestino passenger runs ended in the mid-Seventies, just as the Italian Government dismantled much of their once extensive passenger service.

The Cogedar Line (for Compagnia Genovese d'Armanento) --- absorbed in later years by another Italian, the Costa Line --- used three all-tourist class ships on the Australian trade: the FLAVIA, AURELIA and FLAMINIA. In addition to Genoa and Naples, many of their sailings departed from Bremerhaven, Rotterdam and Southampton.

FAIRSKY   Built 1941
Built by: Western Pipe & Steel Co.,
                San Francisco, California, USA
12,464 gross tons
502 feet long   69 feet wide
Steam turbines geared to single screw
Service speed 18 knots
1461 tourist class passengers

FLAVIA   Built 1947
Built by: John Brown & Co. Ltd.,
                Clydebank, Scotland
15,465 gross tons
556 feet long   70 feet wide
Steam turbines geared to twin screw
Service speed 18 knots
1320 tourist class passengers

[LEFT] Sitmar's FAIRSKY began her sailing career as an auxiliary aircraft carrier in World War II. She concluded her career in the late Seventies as a gambling casino at Manila. [ABOVE] The GUGLIELMO MARCONI and her sistership, the GALILEO GALILEI, were the largest passenger ships ever built for Italy's Lloyd Triestino. Both sailed on the Australian circuit. [BELOW] When economically forced off the North Atlantic, Cunard's MEDIA—a 250 passenger combination ship—was sold to the Italian Cogedar Line and extensively rebuilt for the Australian immigrant trade as the FLAVIA.

Opposite: Michael D.J. Lennon. This page: Roger Sherlock; Skyfotos Limited.

GUGLIELMO MARCONI   Built 1963
Built by: Cantieri Riuniti dell'Adriatico,
                 Monfalcone, Italy
27,905 gross tons
702 feet long   94 feet wide
Steam turbines geared to single screw
Service speed 24 knots
1700 passengers
           300 first class;   1400 tourist class

AMERICAN PRESIDENT LINES

The American President Lines of San Francisco was best known for its PRESIDENT liners, long familiar to Pacific ports. The largest of these --- the PRESIDENTS CLEVELAND, WILSON and ROOSEVELT --- sailed on the trans-Pacific shuttle, between San Francisco, Los Angeles, Honolulu, Yokohama, Kobe, Hong Kong and Manila, then reversing. The combo ships PRESIDENT MONROE and POLK went completely around-the-world for some 96 days, from New York to Panama and Mexico, and then from Califorinia to the Far East, Southeast Asia, India and Pakistan, the Suez and the Mediterranean, and then homewards across the Atlantic.

When the PRESIDENT CLEVELAND and WILSON made their final voyages in 1972, it not only terminated American President liner service but finished off regular cross-Pacific sailings as well. Now, only cruiseships make the occasional journey.

Passenger ship services across most of the world's oceans are in a similar state: most desolate. The great majority of fine ships shown in these pages have long since been put out of work, been lost in the enormous transition to the jet age.

A final meeting in San Francisco Bay in the early seventies between the last trans-Pacific liners, the PRESIDENT WILSON (left) and PRESIDENT CLEVELAND.

American President Lines.

PRESIDENT WILSON   Built 1947/1948
Built by: Bethlehem Alameda Shipyards,
           Alameda, California, USA
19,993 gross tons
609 feet long   76 feet wide
Steam turbo-electric engines geared to twin screw
Service speed 19 knots
684 passengers
          304 first class;   380 economy class